Family Fun
Activity Book

Bob "Captain Kangaroo" Keeshan

Foreword by Anne H. Cohn Donnelly, D.P.H.
Executive Director,
National Committee to Prevent Child Abuse

illustrated by Diane Palmisciano

Fairview Press
Minneapolis, Minnesota

Library of Congress Cataloging-in-Publication Data

Keeshan, Robert.
    Family fun activity book / Bob "Captain Kangaroo" Keeshan ;
illustrated by Diane Palmisciano ; foreword [sic] by Anne H. Cohn
Donnelly.
        p.   cm.
    ISBN 0–925190–29–2
    1. Family recreation.   2. Amusements.   3. Games.   4. Handicraft.
I. Palmisciano, Diane.   II. Title.
GV182.8.K44   1994
790.1'91 -- dc20   94–12353
                                                              CIP

Published by Fairview Press, 2450 Riverside Avenue South,
Minneapolis, MN 55454

Activity research and design by Jay Johnson
Cover art and interior illustrations by Diane Palmisciano
Editorial direction by Pat Samples
Page layout and composition by Circus Design
Cover and interior page design by The Nancekevill Group

First Printing: September 1994
Printed in the United States of America

97 96 95   7 6 5 4 3

For a current catalog of Fairview Press Titles,
please call this toll-free number: 1-800-544-8207

Table of Contents

Age Key

1 =Ages 3-5   **2** = Ages 6-7   **3** =Ages 8-10

Arts & Crafts

Toys & Playsets

Action Games

Quiet(er) Games

Let's Pretend

Nature & Science

Special Note: The Table of Contents indicates one of three age-level recommendations for the activities **1**—Ages 3–5, **2**—Ages 6–7, and **3**—Ages 8–10. These are meant as general guides, but you may discover that children at different stages of development and interest levels may enjoy activities that are recommended for children in an older or younger age group.

Foreword

by Anne H. Cohn Donnelly, D.P.H.

Executive Director, National Committee to Prevent Child Abuse

Have you ever met this four-year-old? He's usually got a great big grin on his face. He laughs easily, he's pretty self-confident, and he relates well to others. It's certainly clear that he cares about others, too. And, he's wonderfully curious.

Chances are when he starts school, he's going to be ready to learn. And when he becomes a teenager, he'll be excited about going to high school. When he graduates from high school, he'll have very positive thoughts about his future. And very likely, as a young adult he will have healthy relationships with others and contribute to society in positive ways.

What kind of family did this little boy come from? Undoubtedly a family filled with love and nurturing. He probably had adults around him who provided a safe and consistent environment and who held him, talked to him, read to him, and played with him. This family was there for him in his earliest years and thereafter.

In 1972, Donna J. Stone, a Chicago philanthropist, became concerned about the children whose families were *not* there for them. Alarmed by the news reports of children suffering serious injuries inflicted by their own parents, she very much wanted to find ways to stop the abuses before children were ever hurt in the first place. She believed deeply that it simply shouldn't hurt to be a child.

Donna's passion and compassion lead to the founding of the National Committee to Prevent Child Abuse (NCPCA). The mission of the NCPCA is to prevent child abuse in all its forms—physical abuse, sexual abuse, neglect and emotional maltreatment.

Donna believed that everyone has a role to play in preventing child abuse. She felt it was important for the NCPCA to help concerned citizens find ways they could contribute to strengthening families. With its national headquarters in Chicago and a network of chapters in fifty states, the NCPCA is leading the nation in child abuse prevention efforts. From one person's vision, a national movement has followed.

Child abuse is an extremely complex problem. Solving it is not easy; a number of different solutions must all be carried out to reduce the number of incidents and their severity. Certainly, the public must be educated about the problem. New parents need to get off to a good start with their babies. They need to know about child development, and they need to develop parenting skills. All parents, particularly those whose lives are filled with the most stress, need people and places to turn to when the challenges of raising their children seem too much to handle. When the big and little stresses of life seem overwhelming, parents need to know how to stop and take time out for themselves. For their part, children need to learn how to protect themselves from abuse and to know what to do if it happens to them. And, above all, families deserve to be supported so they can do a great job of raising healthy, happy children.

One of the main reasons that preventing child abuse today is so very challenging has to do with recent changes in American families. Increasingly, children grow up without having both parents in the home and without grandparents, aunts and uncles nearby. The family simply does not have the extended ties to others who historically helped in raising children. Many more parents work, and are not always at home when children need them. Meanwhile, parents fear that their neighborhoods are becoming unsafe—they wonder and worry about gangs, guns, and drugs. These worries increase the stress that parents feel as they try to juggle the needs of their children, their work, and other community or family obligations. This stress is multiplied many times over for those families also confronting major financial problems, the serious illness of a loved one, dreadful housing conditions, or the addiction of a family member to alcohol or other drugs.

Even as the NCPCA and others develop specific strategies designed to help prevent child abuse (such as intensive home visiting programs for burdened new parents to help them get off to a good start, crisis hotlines, helplines and drop-in centers to aid parents under stress, and parenting classes to prepare young people for the challenging job of being parents), there is much that individual families can do to help themselves. At the top of the list, parents can seek help when they need it—from family members, friends, or professionals. Parents can also learn how their own behavior supports or diminishes their children's well-being. They can stop and listen to the words they use when talking to their children and ask themselves: *Do my words hurt or help?* Also very important for parents is finding ways to create joy and fun in the family. Setting aside time to do things with family members, especially children, can contribute significantly to reducing the burden of stress.

Happy, productive, well-balanced children and young adults don't just happen. They are certainly products of their childhood environment, but even more importantly, they are a reflection of the ways in which they were nurtured. And central to nurturing, as Bob Keeshan points out in this book, is the quality time parents spend with their children. Quality time means interacting with children, involving them, challenging their curiosity, and teaching them what lovable and important people they are. Playing with children is an integral part of quality time. Playing together—not to see who wins, but to learn and grow—is an excellent way for families to make great use of precious time.

If you are an adult reader of this book, you are to be complimented. You understand the value of play. This book should be a useful guide in helping you and your children explore a vast array of creative and fun ways to play together. (If you are a younger person exploring this book, good for you! We hope you will find many great activities to pursue with the adults in your life.)

The world is a complex and often menacing place for children. This book offers a wealth of ideas for creating safe and nurturing times with them. I hope you will use it with this in mind.

An Introduction for Grownups

by Bob Keeshan,
TV's "Captain Kangaroo"

This introduction is intended for those grownups who may have forgotten some of the basic ideas which make being young such an adventure. To adapt to the rigors of the adult world, most of us leave behind those adventures which can make each day in the life of a young person stimulating and exciting.

From infancy, a young person embarks on what I term a "voyage of discovery." As human beings we learn more in the first six years of life than at any other time in human experience. That is why the first ten years or so are so critical to shaping young people intellectually and emotionally. It's a great voyage, and a voyage on which every child needs an "experienced hand," a Captain to serve as a guide through uncharted waters. I have, at times, served as that Captain for many of you, and, with this book, I turn over many of a guide's secrets, in the form of tips for spending enjoyable and productive time with young people.

Every morning Captain Kangaroo tried to keep carrots in his hand and ping pong balls off his head. Dancing Bear would dance as no other bear could dance. Mister

Green Jeans would bring some animals from his amazing menagerie, which would include lambs and lion cubs, small ponies and huge elephants, armadillos and capybaras, slow sloths and swift jaguars, exotic beasts and puppies, kittens and tiny rabbits. (Bunny Rabbit would share a precious carrot with these, but no matter. Before many minutes passed he would trick the Captain out of a new bunch to replenish his supply, which was kept in a vault as secure as the one which sheltered Jack Benny's millions.)

Grandfather Clock would serve as our metronome, ticking away the seconds and minutes of the hour, waking only long enough to recite his latest poem ...

> "Roses are Red
> Violets are blue ...."

The Banana Man would drop by with his fiddle and fruit and Mister Baxter would tell us some stories. The Captain might read from a book telling us about those ducklings in Boston or the secrets of making soup from stones. (Those stories are still being read to children today because, you see, childhood is ageless. Young people today are passing through the same sunlight, the same stormy seas, weathering the same storms and seeing the same rainbows as you once did. If we can remember some of those snapshots from childhood, we will be able to understand the needs of children today.)

Often I would say, at the end of one of Captain's visits, "Mom and Dad, spend some time with your young person today..." Even now, perhaps at one of my lectures, parenting seminars or luncheon speeches, a mother of yesteryear will approach me and talk about what a great idea that was, encouraging parents to spend time with their children. I will reply that many parents, at that time, expressed the same thought, and would add, "But, Captain, what should I do with them?" Grownups, then and now, often find it difficult to spend time with children

because they don't know what to do with that time. In a generation or so, we have surrendered our children to television and video games. The relationship between grownups and children has been altered by busy schedules and because of forgotten secrets, the secrets of guiding children through childhood.

On those occasions when I meet parents, I am often asked, "What is the most important thing I can do for my children?" My answer—"Spend time with them"—is quite general, but always leads to specifics. Some parents feel guilty because they leave their children to earn a living. Why? Because while earning a living benefits

children, our children also need our care and attention. Yes, we may feel tinges of guilt because of the many times we said, "Darling, I'm tired and busy. Go watch television." It can be difficult for today's busy grownups to handle all the demands placed on us. But the one thing that children need above all else is a reasonable amount of our time, time for the building of a relationship, the building of self-esteem, the giving of values, the creation of character. These may seem like rather heavy and serious objectives, and they are, but they can be done in small, incremental ways, the ways that come from spending time, doing whatever, with a child.

This is, if I may say so, a nifty book to reach those objectives. I choose the adjective "nifty" because I want it to sound like fun, which it is. Playing with a child should be enjoyable for a grownup. If a grownup can't enjoy these activities, something is missing, and the goal of child development will be less than it should be. So let it all hang out, remember what childhood was like, and enjoy yourself. Your biggest investment will be your time, and your biggest dividend will be a happy child—happy because of the time you are giving as well as over the activity itself.

In this book you'll find a section called *Arts & Crafts*. These activities are designed to be pretty simple, even for adults; they are *not* a replication of Christmas Eve toy assembly instructions: "Insert Tab E into slot H and fold over…" Pick and choose among them and use the ones that appeal to you, and forget about the rest. Above all, make it fun. Remember the newspaper palm tree your uncle made for you as a kid? It's in here, and nothing could be easier. That look in your young person's eyes as the palms unfold is the same look that was in your eyes umpteen years ago. Or, try the *Smells-Good Ball*—it's easy and smells good, too!

The object of these activities and projects is not to build monuments, but to build character and self-esteem. Self-esteem in a child is built one tiny step at a time. Allow your young person to do things, and not merely watch *you* do them. Show that you have confidence in the ability of the child by allowing him or her to make and discover things. Little by little, the child's confidence will grow, building a tower of self-esteem. The words "I can do it! I can do it!" are a great gift to give a child, and you don't have to embellish them with a red ribbon.

Most toys for children today are so sophisticated that they have no "play value"— they require no imagination, no participation from the child. The activities in this book *demand* the participation of the child and are, therefore, the most ideal kind of toy. They can be educational, like the *Solar System Mobile* or the amazing *Green*

Thumb projects. There is the opportunity to learn about the world around us and its different cultures, as with the *Papier-Mache Wonders* or the *Dinosaur World* projects. Going bonkers on a rainy day? Try *Puzzle Pick Up* or one of my favorites, *Checker Out.*

Trains 'n' Planes reminds me so much of the Treasure House games we would play with a few cardboard boxes, boxes that could take us to a Paris street for *An American in Paris*, a Gershwin adventure, or Villa-Lobos' "Little Train of Capira." The boxes, mixed with fun music and imagination, transport us anywhere in the universe. And you are the grownup accompanying the child on this trip.

I once showed Mister Moose a principle of physics by using the very same materials from *Rocket Power:* "To every action there is an opposite and equal reaction." Important for a young child to learn? Of course not, but a ride on a jet airplane will never be the same. (By the way, Mister Moose was grateful for the physics lesson, and then demonstrated that "to every ping-pong ball falling, there is a Captain to hit!")

It is critical that every child feel a part of "family," have a knowledge of belonging. Reinforce this with the great activities in *Family Pride Projects*—the family photo stand and the family shield. Members of families need to help each other, and the *Family Job Jar* is the perfect way to develop cooperation from every family member—even the youngest. Add the fun items to the job jar and you will be hard-pressed to keep their hand out of it!

Bunny Rabbit, Mister Moose, Mister Green Jeans, and the Captain often played a game that is suggested in this book. We would start with story cards and take turns, each of us continuing a story started by the others. What fun! Needless to say, it is a great game to develop the imagination of a child. At the end, shuffle the cards and begin anew; it's incredible how different stories evolve from the same cards. (We never worried about the imagination of Mister Moose—he had a one-track mind—and in the end, we all ducked!)

This book is filled with ideas for *Arts & Crafts, Action Games, Quiet(er) Games, Let's Pretend, Nature & Science*, and more. It is a Treasure House of imagination, and it's fun to boot. As a grownup, you will be able to recapture the joys of childhood, feel the fresh breeze of spring and lazy summer days. (Fun, yes, but there is nothing lazy about child development.) And who knows—you may also enjoy yourself so very much that we can give you credit for some thorough adult development!

So, folks, spend some time with a young person and enjoy the dividends: a well-developed, secure young person of high self-esteem. Could be we have a doctor, lawyer, or president in the making here. Just remember—*always* remember—none of those career goals is as important as developing a happy child. (Soon to be a happy adult, thanks to you!) Have fun!

Family Fun

Arts & Crafts

Activity Book

Bonker Bubbles

You'll have lots of bubbly, sudsy fun when you mix up a big batch of Bonker Bubbles! It's the perfect outdoor play activity.

What You'll Need:

- dishwashing detergent—
  1 cup; Joy or Dawn are good
  brands to use
- water—3 cups
- corn syrup—3/8 cup
- spoon

- mixing bowl
- cake pan
- empty jar or plastic container—
  with a lid
- bubble blowers (like a pipe
  cleaner, plastic drinking straw,
  or funnel)

Here's How to Make It:

1. Pour the water into a small mixing bowl.

2. Add the detergent and corn syrup to the water. Gently mix the liquids together with a spoon.

3. Let the Bonker Bubbles mix sit for three to five hours before you begin to play with it.

4. Now for some outdoors bubble action! Pour the bubble solution into a cake pan or other shallow container. Dip any kind of bubble maker into the mix. Then, blow through it or wave it around to make some bubbles.

5. Many household items make great bubble makers or bubble blowers. Berry baskets dipped in the bubble mix make many small bubbles when waved around. Funnels, plastic drinking straws, and spools are great bubble pipes. Use your imagination and you'll find lots of bubble maker items in the kitchen—just ask a grownup for some help.

6. Make your own bubble blower from one or more pipe cleaners. Twist the pipe cleaner into a circle shape, leaving room for a handle you can hold onto. The larger the circle, the bigger the bubble. Try bending the pipe cleaner into different shapes, too—any shape will make a great bubble!

7. Store your bubble mix in a glass or plastic container with a lid. The Bonker Bubbles brew should last for weeks of bubble play!

More Family Fun:

Blowing bubbles is fun for the entire family, so gather everyone together for bubbly fun! Remember: Bonker Bubbles is a great out-doors activity, not something you'll want to do in the house. It's messy, and the bubble mix is bad for floors and furniture. So make your bubbles in the yard or the park and, while you're at it, try out these other great bubble ideas:

● Make a Super Bonker Bubbles Blower! Have a grown-up helper remove both ends of three or four empty soup cans with a can opener. Make sure all the ends of the cans are smooth and free of jagged edges! Clean the cans well and dry them thoroughly. Tape them together end-to-end with masking tape. Dip the end of your blower into the bubble mix. Blow through the other end to make a giant bubble!

● Make a Monster Bonker Bubbles Maker! Your grown-up helper can bend a wire coat hanger into a large circle, leaving a handle for you to hold. Wrap masking tape around the sharp end of the handle so it won't poke anyone. Practice dipping the coat hanger into the bubble mix and waving your arm in one smooth motion to make the perfect monster bubble. If the hanger is bent into a circle about six inches round, it will make a bubble the size of a watermelon!

● Play a game with your Bonker Bubbles. Blow a small or big bub-ble that you and a partner can blow back and forth to each other—don't let it pop! Another game variation is "catch," with your partner trying to pop the bubble, catch it in a plastic cup, or pass it through a Bubble Basketball hoop!

4

Quick Play Clay

This kitchen clay dough will last for a long time when you make things and then bake them in the oven! Remember to have a grownup help you with the baking.

What You'll Need:

➤ flour—4 cups
➤ salt—1 cup
➤ alum—1 teaspoon
  (you can find alum at a
  grocery store or drugstore)
➤ water—1 1/2 cups
➤ large mixing bowl

Here's How to Make It:

1. With your hands, mix the ingredients well in a large bowl. If the Quick Play Clay is too dry, add another tablespoon of water and mix it in. Keep kneading the dough until it is smooth and soft.

2. If you want different colors of Play Clay, divide the dough into several parts and use an eyedropper to add one or two drops of food coloring or Color Magic dye (see page 59) to each part. Knead the coloring or dye into each dough part; add more coloring or dye if you want a deeper color to the Play Clay.

3. The Quick Play Clay is now ready to play with! If you're not ready to use all the dough at once, you can put it in a plastic bag or covered container and store it in the refrigerator for as long as two weeks.

4. To make goodies with your Quick Play Clay, lightly flower a counter, table surface, or board and use a rolling pin to roll the dough out flat—about 1/8 inch thick is perfect. Use cookie cutters, jar lids, or other objects to press out shapes—or just use a plastic knife to cut out your own designs. Use a drinking straw dipped in flour to cut out a small hole in the dough (not real close to the edge of your shape). This will allow you to tie a string or fine wire through the hole to hang up your Play Clay creation. The little circles of dough inside the drinking straw can be shaken out and used as decorations, eyes, etc.!

5. Have a grownup help you bake your Quick Play Clay shapes on an ungreased cookie sheet in a 250° Farenheit oven for thirty minutes. Use a spatula to carefully flip the shapes over and bake them for another one and a half hours until they are hard and dry. Take them out of the oven and let them cool.

6. Decorate your Quick Play Clay shapes and ornaments with poster paints or markers. Paint both sides and allow them to dry. With a grownup watching, seal them with brush-on clear nail polish or use a paintbrush and clear shellac.

More Family Fun:

There are many fun uses for Quick Play Clay. Because the baking time in the oven requires the help of a grownup, this is a great whole-family activity. Get everyone involved in making the dough, rolling it out, cutting out shapes, baking, and decorating. Here are some great ideas for your dough:

● Use holiday cookie cutters and make special Easter, Christmas, Kwanza, Channukah, or Valentine's Day decorations to hang up.
● Make a special gift for a grownup—roll out a large circle of dough about one half inch thick and press one of your hands into the center of the dough. Use a pencil to draw your name and the date in the area around the handprint. Use a drinking straw to cut a hole in the top for hanging. Bake it and then paint the area all around your hand so that it really stands out. (Try making a footprint in dough, too.)
● Make party invitations in dough by using a pencil to write the date, time, and place of your party. Cut a hole in the top with a

drinking straw, bake them, paint them, then tie ribbons through the holes and hang each invitation on a friend's doorknob. Ring the bell and wait until someone opens the door—surprise them with the invitation!

● Make lockets, cameos, broaches, or other jewelry items with Quick Play Clay! Use pretty ribbon to hang them around your neck or through a belt or button hole.

● Make a Play Clay sign— "Kathy's Room" or "Danger—My Room Is Dirty!" or any other fun message. Use string or ribbon to hang it around your bedroom doorknob. Make a sign for your bike, your school locker, your garden—use your imagination!

Sculpture Gloop

Pretend to be a famous artist, making amazing statues and make-believe objects with your mysterious Sculpture Gloop! It doesn't take much of anything but your imagination to make something you and your family can really be proud of!

What You'll Need:

- ➤ plaster of paris—one package
- ➤ sand
- ➤ water
- ➤ empty coffee can
- ➤ plastic spoon
- ➤ waxed paper—torn into sheets
- ➤ poster paints
- ➤ paintbrushes
- ➤ craft materials

9

Here's How to Make It:

1. First, make the basic Sculpture Gloop recipe. Put at least one cup of plaster of paris powder in a coffee can. Slowly add water to the plaster of paris and stir it with a plastic spoon. You want the mixture to be well-stirred so it looks like cream.

2. When you have the plaster of paris mixed into a creamy soup, quickly stir in small amounts of sand. You'll want enough sand so that your creamy soup turns thicker, like whipped cream. Mix the sand in fast, though—plaster of paris can dry quickly, so you don't have much time!

3. Pour or scoop out some of your Sculpture Gloop onto a waxed paper sheet. Use the plastic spoon to mold, scoop, round, or pile the Gloop into shapes, figures, squiggles, animals, snakes, towers, or anything you can imagine.

4. You can use your hands to mold and shape the Gloop into a final form. But be quick—remember, the Gloop will begin to harden soon! Add feathers, pipe cleaners, and other craft materials to your sculptures before they harden.

5. When your Gloop has dried completely, use poster paints and other craft materials to finish decorating your sculptures. Let them dry before removing them from the waxed paper.

More Family Fun:

Ask Mom or Dad where you can display your Sculpture Gloop creations so that the world can admire your artistic talents! Here are some more Gloop ideas:

- Have a Gloop sculpting party; make and then award construction paper ribbons for Funniest Gloop, Scariest Gloop, Tallest Gloop, Most Colorful Gloop. Everyone gets a prize!
- Make useful Gloop items like ashtrays, pencil holders, or coin keepers.
- Make Gloop Hearts for Valentine's, Mother's, or Father's Day gifts.
- Build a Gloop Town and make huts, bridges, and other buildings.
- Make Gloop Fun Food—Gloop Burgers, Gloop Ice Cream, Gloop Corn-on-the-Cob. Serve a Gloop Meal to your family and friends!

Pretty Paints

You don't have to be a famous artist to paint something special. Be proud of your projects and show off the artwork that only you can make!

What You'll Need:

- ➤ sugar—3 tablespoons
- ➤ cornstarch—1/2 cup
- ➤ cold water—2 cups
- ➤ food coloring or Color Magic dye (see page 59)
- ➤ dishwashing detergent
- ➤ spoon
- ➤ eyedropper

- ➤ medium pot
- ➤ empty jelly or baby food jars with lids—4 containers for storage
- ➤ old newspapers
- ➤ art smock or old clothes—an old shirt worn backwards makes a great smock

12

Here's How to Make It:

1. With a spoon, mix the sugar and cornstarch together in a medium pot.

2. Stir in water to the sugar/cornstarch mixture. Have a grown-up helper put the pot on low heat over the stove.

3. Keep stirring the mixture over low heat until all the ingredients are blended well.

4. Your grown-up helper can pour equal parts of the mixture into four or five empty jelly or baby food jars (make sure they have lids so you can store the paint after you're done using them).

5. With an eyedropper, add different food coloring or Color Magic dyes to each container of paint. Stir them up with a spoon and keep adding drops of color until you get the color you want.

6. Add a drop of liquid dishwashing detergent to each paint batch and stir it in well. The detergent helps the paint clean up better!

7. Now you're ready to use your Pretty Paints! This is a good finger painting paint, so dip in and spread colors around a sheet of paper. Use a paintbrush or cotton swab if you don't want to use your fingers and hands. For easy clean up, be sure to have old newspapers spread out over the table or on the floor under your artwork.

More Family Fun:

Painting with your fingers or painting with a brush will give you
and your family wonderful new works of art to hang up in your
room or around the house. Here are some more painting fun ideas:

● Use shelf paper to make a long Pretty Paints Mural! Paint a
scene, like a city skyline or a farm. Paint a giant monster. Paint your
friends and family. Paint scenes from a favorite story!

● For extra sparkle, sprinkle some glitter onto your paintings
before they dry!

● Make up a batch of Fat Paint! Stir one cup of flour, one cup of
salt, and one cup of water together in a mixing bowl. Add a few teaspoons of tempera paint and stir the color through the mixture.
Pour the Fat Paint into a plastic squeeze bottle. You can mix up different batches of colors and pour them into different squeeze
bottles, too. Then squeeze the paint out onto paper to make your
paintings. The paint will dry "fat" and puffy, and you can feel the
lines you've drawn with your fingertips!

● Go on a Family Art Outing! Visit a museum, gallery, artist's stu-
dio, or classroom—anyplace where paintings are being made or put
on display.

● Can you try to copy a famous painting using your own Pretty
Paints? It's fun to try! Go to the library with your family and check
out books on paintings and painters. Explore these books and you'll
discover many different art ideas.

Mighty Oobleck

Mysterious Mighty Oobleck isn't really a "craft" because you can't make anything out of it, but it's a simple recipe that's impossible to keep your hands out of. Play with it and see!

What You'll Need:

- ➤ cornstarch—2 cups
- ➤ water—1 cup
- ➤ spoon
- ➤ large mixing bowl or plastic tub

Here's How to Make It:

1 . Mix the cornstarch and water together in a large mixing bowl or plastic tub.

2. Stir the mixture until it starts to thicken. To make a bigger batch of Mighty Oobleck, just keep adding two parts cornstarch to one part water and mix until thick.

3. Now it's time to play with Mighty Oobleck! Keep it over the mixing bowl or over a sink or plastic tub. First, pick it up and squish it between your fingers. The outer edges of the Oobleck are hard and crusty, but when you pick it up, it magically changes into more of a liquidy mush—kind of gross, but lots of fun!

4. Add toys like plastic pails and shovels to scoop up the Mighty Oobleck. Use kitchen utensils like strainers to mash the Oobleck into strange shapes. Make a Mighty Oobleck pie and use mixing spoons, whisks, and other kitchen objects to play with this amazing stuff!

5. With an eyedropper, add drops of food coloring or Color Magic dyes to your Mighty Oobleck and swirl them around!

6. When you're done playing with this mighty mush, clean up all toys, utensils, countertops, bowls, and your hands with soap and water. Wow!

More Family Fun:

It's fun to dig your hands into this amazing and simple-to-make mix! It's fun to feel how oozy and squishy Mighty Oobleck is, too. And when you're done washing the Oobleck down the drain, here are some more touch-and-feel fun projects you and your family can do together:

● Make a Touch-and-Guess Game for your family and friends to play! Just collect a variety of small objects from around the house and put them in paper lunch bags—one object per bag. Players take turns putting their hands into the bags and guessing what the objects are. No peeking is allowed, only touching!

● Try a tasty variation of the Touch-and-Guess Game by putting different foods into bags! Experiment with some of these suggestions: a piece of cooked spaghetti, a grape, a peanut, grains of rice, a radish, a lettuce leaf, and a bread crust.

● Make a Touch-and-Feel booklet or poster using household objects. Tape or glue objects to construction paper and use crayons or markers to label the objects by how they feel. For example: "Soft" for a cotton ball, "Rough" for a piece of sandpaper, "Smooth" for a piece of plastic wrap, "Bumpy" for a piece of corduroy. Turn this project into a game by blindfolding everyone—make them guess what they're feeling by using their sense of touch!

Dinosaur World!

Everybody loves dinosaurs, and you'll have hours of fun playing in a world you can make for your dino friends—complete with an erupting volcano!

What You'll Need:

- sand—in a sandbox or in a foil roaster pan
- empty juice can
- baking soda—1/4 cup
- water—1 cup
- white vinegar—2/3 cup
- dishwashing liquid—1/3 cup
- red food coloring or red Color Magic dye (see page 59)
- eyedropper

- mixing bowl
- spoon
- toy dinosaurs
- sticks
- construction paper
- scissors
- markers or crayons
- tape or glue

Here's How to Make It:

1. Make a large mound of sand in your sandbox, or make a mound of sand in a large foil roasting pan. Think big. This is the Dinosaur World volcano!

2. Put the baking soda into an empty juice can. Make sure the can has been cleaned out and the top removed.

3. Bury the juice can at the top of your sand volcano. Cover the sides with sand right up to the top of the can. This is where the volcano will erupt!

19

4. With a spoon, stir together the water, white vinegar, and dish-washing liquid in a mixing bowl. With an eyedropper, add a few drops of red food coloring or red Color Magic dye. This will make your volcano erupt with red-hot lava (well, not real lava, but it's a fun copy of the real thing)!

5. Decorate your Dinosaur World with toy dinosaurs, twigs, ferns, flowers, rocks, and other objects. You can also use construction paper to draw and cut out prehistoric scenery, dinosaurs, cliffs, rocks, and other objects. Go to the library and check out books on dinosaurs and prehistoric life so that your drawings can look realistic! Color your creations with markers or crayons. You can also color trees and flowers and tape or glue them to sticks which you can place in the sand around your volcano.

6. Now your Dinosaur World is complete. But wait—the volcano has to erupt! Gather your family and friends together and pour the red liquid mixture you made in Step 4 into the juice can containing the baking soda. Watch what happens!

7. Now that your dinos have survived the big volcano blast, you can play with them in your prehistoric park!

More Family Fun:

After your volcano erupts, clean out the juice can, dry it, fill it with more baking soda, and mix up some more red liquid eruption brew! Fun, isn't it? Here are some more fun ideas for other family projects:

● While you're playing with your Dinosaur World creation, have a Prehistoric Picnic or a Prehistoric Party with your family and friends! A grownup can help you make and serve Brontosaurus Burgers, Mastadon Munchies, Velociraptor Veggies, and Jurassic Juice! If it's a birthday party, don't forget to make a Dino Cake!

● Make a Dinosaur Mobile with construction paper dinos that you draw, color, and cut out! Go to a library and check out books on dinosaurs to help you make your dinos realistic. Tape different lengths of string to each dino cutout and attach the strings to a dowel rod or yardstick. Hang up your mobile with another string.

● Go on a Family Dinosaur Outing! Visit a museum, school, or special show where dinosaur bones and exhibits are on display.

● Rent a good dinosaur movie and read books on dinosaurs—there's a lot to learn about the prehistoric past!

Body Beautiful

There's no one quite like you, and here are some special projects that help celebrate how wonderful you really are!

What You'll Need
for a Happy Hands and Funny Feet Mural:

- shelf paper
- finger paints or Pretty Paints (see page 12)—different colors
- cake pans, cookie sheets, or aluminum pie pans—a variety of shallow containers

- old newspapers
- paper towels
- smock, old clothes, or swimwear—an old shirt worn backwards makes a great smock
- crayons or markers

Here's How to Make It:

1. A mural is artwork that you make on a huge sheet of paper, and making a mural is a very messy, very fun project! Because it is messy, it's best to make a Happy Hands and Funny Feet Mural outside, on the sidewalk or patio, for easy clean up. If you choose to do this inside, spread out plenty of old newspapers on a kitchen floor or other hard floor surface—not on carpeting and not close to furniture!

2. You can make this mural alone, or have the fun of making it with friends or family. Everyone should wear old clothes or swimwear. At the very least, wear some type of art smock to protect clothes!

3. Cut one long piece of shelf paper. The length depends on the number of people making the mural. Allow two to three feet of paper for each person making the mural.

4. Now, get out the finger paints and pour a small amount of each color into cake pans, cookie sheets, aluminum pie plates, or other shallow containers. Put only one color into each container. (If you don't want to use store-bought finger paints, have your bunch make some Pretty Paints—see page 12 for instructions.)

5. If you and your fellow mural makers are wearing clothes instead of swimsuits, roll up your sleeves, take off your shoes and socks, and roll up your pant legs. Now for the messy and fun part!

6. A Happy Hands and Funny Feet Mural can only be made up of an assortment of hand and footprints—nothing else! The hand and footprints can be put together to form any kind of design, and they can be any color. Dip your hands and feet into paint and carefully make hand and footprints on the shelf paper. If you want to change paint colors on your hands or feet, you must clean off the old paint first. Use paper towels or a nearby sink or garden hose to do a quick washing. Keep working until the mural is filled with Happy Hands and Funny Feet!

7. Let your mural dry, then have everyone who helped out put their names on the mural with crayons or markers. Display the mural on a wall, fence, door, or window.

What You'll Need for a Body Poser:

➤ shelf paper
➤ posterboard
➤ paste or glue
➤ scissors
➤ construction paper
➤ glitter, fabric scraps, feathers, or other art materials

➤ crayons or markers
➤ paints
➤ paintbrush
➤ old newspapers
➤ brads or metal fasteners— available at stationery stores

Here's How to Make It:

1. Cut a piece of shelf paper. Make it long enough for you to lay down on and still have some extra room.

2. Lie down on your back, on the paper. Keep your arms straight and move them slightly out to the side (but still on the shelf paper), or bend them for a different pose. Relax your legs and spread them out slightly—bend them if you want to. Have a helper use a crayon or a marker to trace an outline of your body on the shelf paper. Don't giggle!

3. With scissors, cut out the shelf paper outline of your body, paste or glue it to a large sheet of posterboard, then cut out the outline again.

4. Carefully cut the arms and legs off your posterboard outline, leaving the body and head area as one big piece. A grownup can help reattach the arms and legs by pressing brads (metal fasteners) through the top of each arm or leg and through the part of the body each connects with. Once the brads have passed through both pieces of posterboard, fold back the two ends. Now the arms and legs on your cutout move for easy posing!

5. Your Body Poser isn't quite done yet—it's time to decorate it! Use markers, crayons, paints, construction paper, and art materials to add facial features, hair, and clothing to the poser. Use your imagination and dress yourself up!

More Family Fun:

It's fun to use your wonderful body to make these fantastic projects! Here are some other great Body Beautiful ideas you and your family might like to try:

● Make a Happy Family or a Best Friends Mural! Cut a piece of shelf paper for each member of your family or your friends. Make each piece long enough for the person to lay down on and still have some extra room. Line up the papers side-by-side so that all the bottom edges of the sheets are lined up together and all the sides touch. Now have everyone lie down on their backs on their sheets of paper. All the feet should line up evenly. Have everyone spread their hands out so they're touching their neighbor's hands. Have helpers trace the outline of each body. Then tape all the sheets together into one long mural—with everyone holding hands! Everyone should decorate their own bodies (see the Body Poser ideas above), then sign their names next to their pictures. Hang up your mural in a special place!

● Have your family or friends each make their own Body Posers. Use the Body Posers like giant puppets to put on a show or dance to special music!

● Go to the library and check out books on the amazing human body. Learn all about what makes bodies work and how to keep your body healthy. And learn about good touch and bad touch—know how to tell a grownup you can trust if anyone touches you in a bad way!

Hotstuff Play Clay

Why is this called "hotstuff?" Because this is a fun play dough recipe that you and your grown-up helper can cook together on top of the stove. When it cools down, you're ready to make something!

What You'll Need:

- flour—2 cups
- salt—1/2 cup
- cream of tartar—4 tablespoons
- water—2 cups
- oil—2 tablespoons
- food coloring or Color Magic dye (see page 59)—4 teaspoons
- spoon
- medium pot
- plastic container with lid or airtight plastic bag

Here's How to Make It:

1. With a spoon, mix the flour, salt, and cream of tartar in a medium cooking pot.

2. Stir in the water, food coloring or Color Magic dye, and oil. Mix all the ingredients well.

3. Now a grownup can help you cook the Hotstuff Play Clay. Put the cooking pot with your clay recipe on medium heat over the stove. Stir the dough while it cooks for three to five minutes. You'll know the dough is ready when it starts to come away from the sides of the pan and form a big ball that's hard to stir.

4. Turn out the dough ball onto a countertop or cutting board that's been lightly sprinkled with flour. Let the dough cool.

5. Knead the dough until it gets nice and smooth. Now you're ready for some Hotstuff Play Clay fun! This homemade recipe will make the same projects as the expensive clay from a store.

6. Store your dough in covered plastic containers or sealed plastic bags. If the dough dries out, add a few drops of oil or water to it and knead well. The dough will be soft and smooth again!

7. Make more batches of Hotstuff Play Clay and add different food coloring or Color Magic dyes to each batch. Now you can make rainbow-colored projects!

More Family Fun:

Hotstuff Play Clay is fun for the entire family to make! But cooking things on the stove isn't the only fun you and your family can find in the kitchen. Ask a grownup how you can help in other activities around the kitchen: washing and drying dishes, cleaning and scrubbing vegetables, sweeping the floor, setting the table, and cooking meals. It's fun to help! And it's fun to make lots of projects with your dough:

● Roll out your Hotstuff Play Clay with a rolling pin. Use cookie cutters, a jar lid, toothpick, drinking straw, bottle cap, paper clip (but not for children under four years old!), and other utensils to make interesting shapes and patterns in your dough.

● Put the dough into a garlic press and see what you can make!

● Press a piece of dough onto comics from the newspaper. Lift it off and you've got a copy of the picture on your dough! Stretch it out to make the picture look funny.

● Roll out the dough into long tubes. Make snakes or roll up the tubes and make pots, vases, or bowls. Press macaroni pieces into the dough to decorate your creations!

Pretty Paste

I t's fun to make a colorful, gooey paste that you can use in many craft and gift projects. And when the Pretty Paste dries, it looks like stained glass!

What You'll Need:

- ➤ white liquid glue
- ➤ food coloring or Color Magic dye (see page 59)
- ➤ spoon
- ➤ eyedropper
- ➤ small bowl
- ➤ pipe cleaners

- ➤ waxed paper
- ➤ piece of foam, play dough, or clay
- ➤ art smock or old clothes—an old shirt worn backwards makes a great smock

31

Here's How to Make It:

1. Spread out waxed paper sheets to cover a tabletop or other work surface.

2. Pour the liquid white glue into a small bowl. You'll need at least a half inch of glue for this project.

3. Use an eyedropper to add drops of food coloring or Color Magic dye. With a spoon, stir the color into the glue and mix well. Add more drops of coloring or dye to the glue to get just the color you want.

4. Repeat Steps 2 and 3 above to make different color batches of Pretty Paste. It's fun to have three or more colors to work with!

5. Take a pipe cleaner and bend part of it into a shape. Use the rest of it as a stem to hold onto when you dip your shape into the Pretty Paste. The shape must be a completely enclosed design, so be sure to wrap the end of the pipe cleaner around the stem to close the shape. You can make a heart, a circle, an oval, a flower petal, or any shape you want. Wrap another pipe cleaner onto the end of the stem if you want a longer stem—maybe for a fairy wand or a flower!

6. Next, hold onto the pipe cleaner stem and dip your shape into the Pretty Paste. Completely cover the pipe cleaner and the shape with the paste. Pull it out and hold it over the bowl until the glue stops dripping from the pipe cleaner. A colorful film will form inside your pipe cleaner shape, like the film you see when you dip a bubble wand into bubble mix. If the film pops, carefully dip the pipe cleaner into the glue again. If the Pretty Paste becomes too thick and sticky, stir in a few drops of water.

7. On the waxed paper, gently lay the pipe cleaner on its side to dry. Or you can stick the stem into a piece of foam, play dough, or clay.

8. The Pretty Paste shapes will be dry in about one hour. Now, that was easy!

More Family Fun:

Pretty Paste projects are simple to make, so they're great for very young children. But they're also beautiful when they're finished, so every member of the family will enjoy them! Here are some great Pretty Paste project ideas:

● Make a flower arrangement or bouquet! Form a tulip shape from a single pipe cleaner and add another pipe cleaner to make a long stem. Dip leaf shapes into green Pretty Paste and wrap the pipe cleaner leaves around the flower stems. You can dip separate petal shapes into Pretty Paste and wrap them on the end of a pipe cleaner stem to form a single flower. Add leaves to the stem. Place your flowers in a decorated juice can, paper cup, or May Day basket!

● Make a Pretty Paste bouquet of heart-shaped flowers for a Valentine's Day, Mother's Day, Father's Day, or birthday present! It's a great way to say "I love you" to your family.

● Make window decorations. After you bend your pipe cleaner into a shape for dipping into the paste, bend the remaining length of the pipe cleaner into a loop. Run a string or ribbon through the loop and hang up your decoration against a window. It will look beautiful when the sun shines through it!

● Use your imagination and make Pretty Paste dress-up jewelry! Try making hook-on earrings, brooches, lockets, charms, rings, and other items.

So-Big Family Tower

Here's another family pride activity. Everyone in the family can get creative and help build a So-Big Family Tower!

What You'll Need:

- ➤ milk cartons—4 or more; use the half-gallon size
- ➤ white or brown wrapping paper, construction paper, or old grocery bags
- ➤ markers or crayons
- ➤ art materials— glitter, white liquid glue, fabric scraps, etc.
- ➤ tape or glue
- ➤ scissors
- ➤ sand or rocks

Here's How to Make It:

1. Get one empty milk carton for each member of your family. Rinse out and dry the cartons before you begin.

2. Have a grown-up helper cut off the tops and the bottoms of all but one milk carton. one milk carton will be the base of your So-Big Family Tower—only cut off the top of that milk carton!

3. Cut pieces of plain white or brown wrapping paper, construction paper, or old grocery bags to the height of each milk carton. Now wrap the paper around the milk carton and cut it so the ends overlap. Tape the paper snugly to each milk carton.

4. Give one milk carton to each member of the family. Family members should decorate their milk cartons with special things about themselves and about the family! Use crayons, markers, paints, or art materials to decorate the four sides of each milk carton with anything you'd like: pictures, animals, words, colors, shapes, self-portraits, your house, your car, your favorite food, scenes from family events (like a holiday, special present, close call, new house, new baby). (You can also use paints and paint brushes to decorate, but be sure to spread out plenty of old newspapers and wear old clothes or art smocks.)

5. Here's one more step for a grown-up helper. At the open ends of the milk cartons, cut a two-inch slit along each of the corners (four slits on the top and four on the bottom).

6. Put some sand or rocks in the milk carton base (the one that still has a bottom) so that it is weighted down and can support the rest of the So-Big Family Tower. Have each family member slide their cartons onto the tower, connecting the slits in the corners and notching the cartons snugly together. Look at the tower now—it's So Big!

More Family Fun:

Your family is special, and your So-Big Family Tower can show the world how different and special each member of the family is! Here are some other projects you can make to show your family pride:

● Everyone in your neighborhood can make a So-Big Family Tower. Have a big neighborhood party and bring all the towers for decoration! After the party, all the families can display their towers on their own front porch or in their yard.

● The So-Big Family Tower is a great project for everyone at a Family Reunion or special family gathering, such as picnics, weddings, after school, after a meal or after church! Have everyone decorate a milk carton for the So-Big Family Tower. Keep adding milk carton levels to the tower and see how high you can make it.

● Use poster board or construction paper to make a Family Calendar! A grownup can help you draw lines on the paper to make a calendar grid. Fill in the numbers for the current month. Decorate the daily boxes with pictures of special family times: holidays, birthdays, outings, family meetings, appointments, school events, reunions, parties, trips. Make a new calendar every month.

Magic Beanstalk

Jack and the Beanstalk is a great story, and now you can make Jack's Magic Beanstalk using just a little imagination and some old newspapers!

What You'll Need:

➤ old newspapers
➤ tape
➤ scissors
➤ dried beans—
　just a few!

Here's How to Make It:

1. Lay one sheet of newspaper flat on the floor or on a table.

2. Roll the newspaper at one end to the crease at the center of the page. Make sure to roll the newspaper loosely, not tight!

3. Lay a second sheet of newspaper over the first one. Lay it down so it starts at the center crease of the first paper and covers the unrolled half.

4. Keep rolling the newspaper—loosely—down to the center crease in the second sheet of newspaper.

5. Lay another sheet of newspaper down, again starting at the center crease and covering the unrolled half of the paper.

6. Loosely roll up the paper to the center crease, add another paper, keep rolling, and keep adding newspaper sheets. Roll five to ten sheets of newspaper in all.

7. When you have enough sheets, finish rolling up the newspaper. Tape the loose end so that you make a newspaper tube.

8. With scissors, cut four slits at one end of the newspaper tube. Make each slit about four inches long.

9. Put your fingers down into the newspaper roll—the end you cut the slits in— and start to pull out the center of the roll. As you pull, also twist the newspaper tube at the same time (it makes it easier to unroll the newspaper tube).

10. Keep pulling and twisting...pulling and twisting...pulling and twisting. And watch your Magic Beanstalk grow...and grow...and grow!

More Family Fun:

Here are some fun ideas you can try out with your Magic Beanstalk:

● Go with your family to the library and check out the story of Jack and the Beanstalk. Get your friends together and act out the story. Use some dried beans as a prop. Throw them on the ground, then bring out your newspaper tube and show your audience how Jack grew a Magic Beanstalk!

● Make a lot of Magic Beanstalks and stand them up in empty coffee cans filled with sand. Now you have a Magic Forest that you and your friends can play in!

● Play dress-up and use your beanstalks as Magic Wands, Swords, Lasers, or Walking Sticks!

● Hold a beanstalk in each hand, and you have magically become a Bird—flap your newspaper wings and fly around the yard!

Stained Glass Pictures

Stained glass is beautiful in the windows of churches and old homes. Here's an easy way to make your own pictures that will have a stained glass look!

What You'll Need:

- ➤ white paper—1 sheet
- ➤ old newspapers
- ➤ waxed paper—2 sheets, cut to the same size
- ➤ dried flowers and leaves
- ➤ crayons

- ➤ pencil or crayon sharpener
- ➤ glitter, metallic confetti, yarn, or other art materials
- ➤ clothes iron

Here's How to Make It:

1 . First, collect one or two beautiful flowers, leaves, or ferns and place them between the pages of a big book. Stack more heavy books on top of this book. Let your natural items press out flat and dry for ten days. Now they're ready for this project!

2. Lay an old newspaper down on a table or other work surface. Lay a sheet of white paper on top of the newspaper. Then lay a sheet of waxed paper on top of the sheet of white paper.

3. Arrange your dried flowers, leaves, or ferns on the waxed paper.

4. Take off the paper wrapping from several colorful crayons. Sharpen the crayons with a pencil or crayon sharpener. Sprinkle the crayon shavings over the flowers, leaves, or ferns and sprinkle them on other areas of the waxed paper.

5. Arrange other art materials in your picture—add colorful threads from fabric samples, yarn, decorative lace, glitter, metallic confetti shapes—anything you have will work.

6. Lay the second sheet of waxed paper on top of your finished artwork.

7. Have a grownup help you with the ironing part. Set a clothes iron on a low temperature. Seal the two sheets of waxed paper together by ironing over your picture and melting the crayons. Hang your Stained Glass Picture on a wall or refrigerator, or tape it up on a window and let the sun shine through it!

8. For a different effect, leave out the dried flowers, leaves, or ferns. Sharpen peeled crayons and make little piles of colored shavings. On a sheet of waxed paper, arrange pieces of yarn in designs, patterns, pictures, or words. Then fill in the areas around the yarn with crayon shavings until the waxed paper is completely covered (just leave a little space around the edges). Place the second sheet of waxed paper over the shavings and seal them with a clothes iron set on low. There you have it—another beautiful Stained Glass Picture!

More Family Fun:

Stained Glass Pictures make great decorations and gifts! Here are some other fun ideas you might also like to try:

● Cut the waxed paper pieces into smaller circles that can be hung with string or ribbon as decorations for windows, lockers, doorknobs, or bikes. Add a special person's photograph and make a Stained Glass Locket. Circle-shaped Stained Glass Pictures also make great drink coasters!

● Make a set of Stained Glass Placemats for every member of your family! Personalize the mats with each person's favorite colors and flowers. Cut out pieces of yarn to spell out their names, too.

● Go on a Family Nature Outing! Take a hike, plan a picnic, go camping, climb some hills or visit a farm, nature preserve, park, or beach area. Collect flowers, leaves, ferns, grasses, and other natural items for drying—use them in new Stained Glass Pictures. Don't pick flowers or other items in public parks, on private property, or in other areas which are not to be disturbed.

Mosaic Marvels

A mosaic is a picture or a design you can make by placing small pieces of different colored materials together. Most mosaics are made with pieces of stone or glass—but your special mosaic pictures will be made with colored popcorn and eggshells!

What You'll Need:

- ➤ popping corn
- ➤ popcorn popper or pot with lid
- ➤ cooking oil—if needed for popping the corn
- ➤ water
- ➤ food coloring or Color Magic dye (see page 59)
- ➤ cups or small bowls— 1 for each color

- ➤ spoon
- ➤ fork
- ➤ paper towels
- ➤ paper or posterboard
- ➤ pencil
- ➤ white liquid glue
- ➤ white eggshells—from 12 eggs

Here's How to Make It:

1. Have a grownup help you pop some popping corn. Follow the directions that come with the popping corn. Use either a popcorn

popper (with or without cooking oil, as required) or use a pot with a lid and some cooking oil. Okay, eat some of the popcorn, too, but be sure to save some for your mosaic!

2. Pour some water into small cups or bowls, one container for each color you'd like to dye the popcorn. With an eyedropper, add drops of food coloring or Color Magic dye to the water and stir with a spoon. Add more drops until you get the color you want.

3. Place a few popcorn kernels into one of the colors. Use a spoon to stir the popcorn around the water—but stir it just once and quickly take the kernels out and place them on paper towels to dry. Wait until the popcorn completely dries before using it with your mosaic.

4. Instead of popcorn, you can also use eggshells! Save the shells from twelve white eggs. Wash them well and place them on paper towels to dry. Now for the fun part—smash the dried eggshells into tiny pieces with a spoon (smash them on a dishtowel). Place equal

47

amounts of the eggshell pieces in the cups or bowls filled with colored water and let them soak up the color for about fifteen minutes. Take the shells out of the colors with a fork and lay them out on paper towels. Let them dry overnight before using them with your mosaic.

5. Draw a design on a sheet of paper or posterboard with a pencil.

6. If you're using colored popcorn, fill in different areas of your design with liquid white glue. Fill in the glued area with the popcorn kernels. Continue to lay down more glue and more popcorn until your mosaic is finished! Let it dry overnight.

7. If you're using colored eggshells, glue each eggshell piece directly to the paper or posterboard. Keep gluing eggshells beside each other until the entire picture is made! Let it dry overnight, too.

More Family Fun:

Old popcorn that's too stale to eat is great for coloring and making mosaic pictures with! And don't throw away your eggshells, either! Recycle them in beautiful mosaic pictures. Here are some more ideas:

● Make beautiful jewelry from colored popcorn kernels! With a needle and thread, string colored popcorn kernels together to make bracelets, necklaces, and headbands.

● Make long strands of colored popcorn with a needle and thread and hang them as colorful garlands on your family Christmas tree!

● Popcorn was a gift to all people from the Native Americans. They planted corn in their fields before the first European settlers sailed to North America! Go to the library with your family and check out books on Native Americans, their history, their way of life, and their many other gifts to the world.

● Have a Family Movie Night! Rent some favorite movies, pop some popcorn, and have everyone snuggle together and watch movies. Be sure to have plenty of blankets, quilts, pillows, sleeping bags and cushions on hand, along with the popcorn, juice, and other treats.

● Make mosaic pictures out of small pieces of torn or cut-up construction paper! Glue the small scraps of colored paper together to form a picture.

● Make mosaic pictures out of macaroni and other small dry noodles! Decorate the noodles with poster paints, let them dry, then glue them together on paper to form a picture.

Going to Seed

You may not realize it, but a tiny seed is quite powerful. It's food for birds and other animals, it grows plants to feed the world—and it makes great craft projects, like Birdseed Baubles and the Seedy Pencil Holder!

What You'll Need for Birdseed Baubles:

- white liquid glue
- waxed paper
- birdseed
- cup or small bowl
- spoon
- plastic bag or baggie
- string

Here's How to Make Them:

1. Take off the cap on a bottle of liquid white glue. On a sheet of waxed paper, carefully squeeze out a squiggly trail of glue—you can make any design you'd like! Try not to squeeze out too much glue. Avoid lumpy clumps of glue in your baubles and designs.

2. Pour some birdseed in a cup or small bowl. With your fingers, slowly sprinkle birdseed over your glue design—make sure you cover all the glue with birdseed!

3. Let your Birdseed Bauble dry overnight.

4. When it's dry, tilt the waxed paper and let the extra birdseed fall off your bauble into a plastic bag or baggie. You can save this seed for another project...or you can feed the birds!

5. Slowly peel off the waxed paper from the Birdseed Bauble. Tie a string around the bauble and hang it up on the wall or in a window!

*What You'll Need
for a Seedy Pencil Holder:*

➤ seeds—melon, sunflower, bird, or spice seeds

➤ empty coffee can

➤ construction paper

➤ scissors

➤ white liquid glue

➤ paper cup

➤ paintbrush

➤ tape

➤ old newspapers

Here's How to Make It:

1. Cut a piece of construction paper as tall as an empty coffee can and long enough to more than fit around the can.

2. Spread old newspapers out on your table or work surface. Lay the construction paper down on the newspapers.

3. Pour some liquid white glue into a paper cup. With a paintbrush, paint a section of the construction paper strip with some glue. You can paint a stripe or a squiggly, wavy area. Paint a design, if you'd like. Just leave about one half inch at each end of the strip—later, you're going to tape these ends together around the coffee can.

4. Cover the glue with one kind of seed. Tilt the paper strip and shake off any loose seeds.

5. Keep painting other sections of the construction paper strip with glue. Cover these sections with different seeds and shake off the loose seeds. Again, make sure you leave about one half inch at each end of the strip.

6. Let the construction paper strip dry overnight.

7. Gently curve the paper strip around the coffee can. Overlap the ends of the strip and tape them together. Paint the last section of the paper strip with glue and cover it with seeds. Shake off the loose seeds and let it dry. Your Seedy Pencil Holder is ready!

More Family Fun:

Seeds plus a few other materials make great craft projects. Your finished projects will make good gifts, decorations, and useful household items. Here are some other "seedy" ideas:

- Make a Birdseed Bauble that spells out your name or the name of a friend or family member!
- Make flowers with construction paper petals and pipe cleaner stems. Put this craft bouquet in your Seedy Pencil Holder—what a special gift!
- Have a Family Seed Outing! Go to a grocery store, nursery, garden supply shop, or discount store and pick out a variety of flower and vegetable seeds for your home garden. You and your family can plant a special garden in your yard or in indoor pots.
- Go to the library with your family and check out books on seeds, flowers, vegetables, gardening, and other growing subjects! Learn how to take care of your own plants.

Family Job Jar

This craft project magically turns doing good things around the home into a fun game for the whole family!

What You'll Need:

- ➤ empty glass jar or coffee can
- ➤ construction paper
- ➤ scissors
- ➤ tape, paste, or glue
- ➤ markers, crayons, or colored pencils
- ➤ glitter, fabric scraps, feathers, or other art materials
- ➤ old magazines
- ➤ pen or pencil
- ➤ old newspapers

Here's How to Make It:

1. Cut a piece of construction paper as tall as an empty glass jar or coffee can and long enough to more than fit around the jar or can.

2. Spread old newspapers out on your table or work surface. Lay the construction paper down on the newspapers.

3. Decorate the construction paper strip. Since this is a Job Jar, you might want to print that on the strip. Use art materials, crayons, markers, and other materials to make it special! Try cutting out pictures from old magazines that show household job items—a broom, furniture polish, a pile of laundry, a trash can, or food on a plate.

4. Gently wrap the decorated construction paper strip around the jar or coffee can. Overlap the ends of the strip and tape or glue them together. The outside of your Job Jar is done! Now for the inside…

5. Cut up about twenty small slips of construction paper—make them small, about one half inch tall and two inches long.

6. Sit down with your family and talk about different jobs everyone can do at home. With a pen or pencil, write down one job or way to help the family on each slip of paper. Write no more than ten jobs down. Put the slips into your Job Jar.

7. Besides jobs, also talk about special things that are fun to do with other members of your family. These could also be special treats for helping out around the home. Write down one special treat or fun thing to do on each slip of paper. Write no more than ten treats down. Put the slips into your Job Jar. Make sure you have the same number of job and treat slips!

8. Talk with your family about how to use the Job Jar. Look for some ideas under "More Family Fun." Once everyone agrees on how and when to use the Job Jar, put the jar in a special place, such as on top of the refrigerator or in your room. When the time comes for you to use the jar with a grownup, reach inside—no peeking!—and pull out a slip of paper. Is it a job or is it a treat? Keep pulling out slips of paper until you have one job and one treat. Here's the Big Job Jar Rule: First you do the job and help out; then you may have the treat!

9. Have a Family Meeting once a week. During or just after a family meal is the best time for these meetings. Talk about the job and treat slips in your Job Jar. Are there new jobs you can help out with around the home? Are there new treats you'd like or new things that you would like to do? You might want to take some things out of your jar, so talk this over with your family. Cut out more construction paper slips, write down one job or one treat on each slip, and add them to your Job Jar. Remember to keep the same number of job and treat slips!

More Family Fun:

Here are some of the things that can make the Job Jar a great addition to your family:

● Some ideas for jobs to write down for your Job Jar: make a bed, empty a wastebasket, collect old newspapers for recycling, put silverware into the dishwasher, dust furniture in one room, clear dishes off the table, be Kitchen Helper for a dinner meal, pick up all toys around the house, sweep the back steps, sharpen pencils.
● Some ideas for treats to write down for your Job Jar: a second helping of dessert, a favorite movie to rent, a story read to you by someone special, an activity of your pick from this book, a trip to the library, a trip to the park or zoo (or another special outing), a new

coloring book or small toy, a friend invited over for dinner, a board game or sport to play, a dinner or recipe that you get to pick out.

● Some families have special rules about Job Jars. You and your family can make up your own rules, but here are some suggestions:

— A certain day of the week is "Job Day." Everyone pitches in and helps around the house during that day. Everyone works together for a certain amount of time.

— Older children can share the same Job Jar with grownups. Younger children should have their own Job Jars with special things that they can do to help out.

— Some families set time limits for giving treats, like getting the treat during the week after you do your job.

— When you do a job, do it well! It's important to try your best.

— When you finish a job, have a grown-up check what you did. It's special to hear a grownup say, "Great job!" when you're finished.

● Double the fun of this project by making two jars, one for "Jobs" and one for "Treats."

Color Magic

Here's a fun and easy recipe to make a safe, non-toxic coloring dye that has some great craft uses. Make a big batch of Color Magic dyes and you can store them for future projects, too.

What You'll Need:

- crepe paper streamers—3 or 4 colors, several feet of each color
- paper cups
- lukewarm water
- empty jelly or baby food jars with lids—for storage
- scissors
- art smock or old clothes— an old shirt worn backwards makes a great smock
- old newspapers

Here's How to Make It:

1. First, lay down lots of old newspaper or an old plastic tablecloth so your Color Magic dyes won't stain the surface you work on.

2. Fill each paper cup half full with cut-up pieces of crepe paper—put only one color in each cup. For a lighter dye, fill the cup almost full with lukewarm water. For a darker dye, add only enough water to cover the crepe paper in the cup.

3. Let your Color Magic dye "brew" a little bit—it just takes a few minutes. Then squeeze the crepe paper into each cup and throw out the wet paper. You now have a dye the color of the crepe paper!. Store the dye in empty jelly or baby food jars. Now you're ready for the Color Magic fun to begin!

4. Use your new color dyes to "watercolor" beautiful, soft pictures and designs on paper towels or white paper—a cotton swab makes a great brush. Use a new swab for each color so you don't mix colors into a muddy mess. Experiment with the dyes by mixing primary colors (red, yellow, and blue) and making new color combinations—take an eye dropper and slowly add two different colors into a new storage jar to make more colors!

5. Use a new household sponge as a stencil! Cut out a shape from the sponge and pour a small amount of dye into a saucer. Dip your sponge stencil in the dye, then "stamp" out your shape on a piece of paper, a T-shirt, or a paper towel. Use the stencil to repeat the pattern or make great designs. When you're done using one color of dye, rinse the sponge stencil clean and dry it before you use a different color. Cut out suns and moons and stars, animals, alphabet letters, hearts and other shapes, or leaves and other nature patterns.

6. Add Color Magic dye to the Hotstuff Play Clay recipe (see page 28) or the Quick Play Clay recipe (see page 5) to make different colored modeling doughs!

7. Try decorating a plain white T-shirt with your new dyes. Use cotton swabs or water color brushes to apply small amounts of the dyes. You'll need to do a little experimenting at first—for example, don't make big wet splotches, or they'll completely soak through the fabric and color the other side of the T-shirt. The color will wash out of most fabrics, so your designs might not last forever—but it's fun to wear your own art creations!

8. Use Color Magic dye to decorate hard-boiled white eggs, just like the store-bought dyes for Easter eggs. First, you might want to decorate the eggs with designs or words by drawing on the shells with a white crayon (the dye will skip over the crayon lines). Then soak the eggs in cups or bowls filled with dye until the shells take on the color. Use a spoon to scoop the eggs out of the dye. Let the eggs dry thoroughly before handling. Try filling cups or bowls with enough dye to cover only half the egg shells—you can make great two-toned eggs that way!

More Family Fun:

Here are more fun things to do with your Color Magic dyes:

- Hang up dried Color Magic pictures in your room or stick them up on the refrigerator with magnets.
- Have your family model their colorful new T-shirts.
- Get a grownup to help you hard-boil some eggs, then you can decorate and color them—let everyone have one of your egg-stra special treats for a nutritious lunchtime snack!

(Remember, always wear a smock or old clothes when you do craft projects with this coloring dye; it washes out of most fabrics, but it's still best to protect your clothing!)

Family Pride Projects

I t's great to be proud of your family! These craft ideas are sure to make everyone happy and pleased to be related to you.

What You'll Need for a Family Photo Stand:

➤ posterboard—1 or 2 pieces; 5 inches tall and 8 inches wide
➤ pencil
➤ scissors
➤ markers or crayons
➤ art materials—glitter, white liquid glue, fabric scraps, etc.
➤ tape or glue

Here's How to Make It:

1. Fold the posterboard in half lengthwise.

2. Open the poster board up and lay it flat again, with the back fold facing up. Fold each side in half, toward the back fold. Now you've got three folds that will make the posterboard stand up like an accordion.

3. With a pencil, draw a shape in the top portion of each of the four folded sections of the posterboard. Cut out the shapes with scissors.

4. Gather four photographs of your family, including pets. The photos should be small, or ones you can cut to fit the Family Photo Stand. (Ask permission before you cut a photo!) The photos should be larger than the openings you've cut in the stand. Center the pictures in the cutout shapes, then tape them to the back of the stand so they show through the cutouts.

5. To make your Family Photo Stand more sturdy, cut and fold another piece of posterboard the same size as the stand and tape or glue it to the back of the first piece of posterboard.

6. Decorate the Family Photo Stand with markers, crayons, glitter, and other art materials. Draw borders around the photographs that peek out through the cutouts. Make designs, draw flowers—be colorful and creative. Set up the stand on top of a table, bookshelf, piano, or desk. Give it to someone in your family as a special present!

What You'll Need for a Family Shield:

- ➤ posterboard
- ➤ dinner plate
- ➤ pencil
- ➤ scissors

- ➤ markers or crayons
- ➤ art materials—glitter, white liquid glue, fabric scraps, etc.
- ➤ tape or glue

Here's How to Make It:

1. Make a special Family Shield, decorated with a picture that represents your family! First, using a pencil and a dinner plate, trace a circle on a piece of posterboard. Cut out the circle. If you don't have posterboard, a paper plate makes a great shield, too!

2. Use markers, crayons, and art materials to make a picture you think represents your family. Draw anything—hearts, flowers, pictures of each member of your family, pets, your house, a rainbow. Write the last name of your family on the shield and add a decorative border, too!

3. When you're finished, hang up your Family Shield in a special place of honor! This makes a great keepsake for your family and is a fun project to make at a family birthday party or reunion.

More Family Fun:

Each family is different and special, and your Family Photo Stand and Family Shield can show the world how special your family is! Here are some other projects you can make to show your family pride:

● Everyone in your neighborhood can make a Family Shield. Tape the back of the shields to yardsticks or rulers and you can have a Family Parade—hold your shields up high, march around the block, then have a big neighborhood party!

● Cut out a triangle shape from an old sheet or pillowcase and make a Family Flag! Decorate it with a family picture using fabric paints. Or use fabric markers and try tie-dying the flag for extra color (see page 71).

● Make a Family Tree! Find a short tree branch and stick it upright into a small mound of play dough or clay. Cut out large leaf shapes from construction paper. Write the names of your family members on one side of the leaves and tape or paste photographs of them to the other side (or draw a picture with crayons). Include pets if you like. Tape the leaves to the branch and proudly display your strong, growing family! Keep adding cousins, aunts, uncles, newborn babies, and other family members to the tree, including your ancestors!

Windy Music

Make a great gift for someone special in your family—easy-to-make Wind Chimes that you can hang up outside to make beautiful music!

What You'll Need:

- ➤ dowel rod, broomstick, or a stick—1 foot long or longer
- ➤ empty cans—4; different sizes
- ➤ metal spoons, large or small—4
- ➤ large nail
- ➤ hammer
- ➤ string—5 pieces; (four 1-foot pieces and one 2-foot piece)
- ➤ scissors
- ➤ poster paints
- ➤ paintbrush
- ➤ art smock or old clothes—an old shirt worn backwards makes a great smock

Here's How to Make It:

1. Make your Wind Chimes with large and small tin cans, metal spoons, or mixing spoons. Cans and spoons make different sounds when they bump into each other in the wind. Cans clink and clang, spoons tinkle and sound a little more musical. Pick which kind of chimes you want to make—separate can and spoon chimes, or a set of chimes that uses two spoons and two cans!

2. If you're using cans, clean them out thoroughly. Have a grown-up helper make sure there are no sharp ends left around the open top of each can. Soak the cans in warm water until the paper labels peel off. You just want the metal to show! Make sure the cans are completely dry before you begin.

3. If you'd like, use poster paints to decorate the cans. Wear an art smock or old clothes if you're painting. Think of music and nature and beautiful colors when you paint pictures or designs on the cans!

4. With a hammer and a big nail, have your grown-up helper punch a hole in the bottom of each can, right in the center.

5. With scissors, cut a 1-foot piece of string for each can or spoon you'll be using on your Wind Chimes. Pass a string through the hole in the bottom of each can and tie a knot in the end of the string that's inside the can—the knot will keep the string from slipping out! If you're using spoons, tightly tie the end of the string around the spoon (or loop it through the hole in the end of a metal mixing spoon and tie it tightly).

6. Tie the other end of the strings to a dowel rod, broomstick, or stick. Make sure the stick you're using is one foot or longer. Space each item about two and one half inches apart. This gives the chimes room to swing in the wind and hit against each other to make music! Try to hang no more than four items on any one set of chimes.

7. Tie a two-foot piece of string to the dowel, broomstick, or stick and hang up the Wind Chimes on your front porch, balcony, or a tree in your yard. You may need to move the string off-center to make sure your Wind Chimes are properly balanced. An easy option is to tie your chimes to a wire coat hanger—it even has its own handle for hanging. Now wait for the wind to blow, and listen to the music!

More Family Fun:

- Make bigger Wind Chimes by adding more cans and spoons! You can even tie two or more dowels or sticks together and make a Wind Chimes Mobile!

- What makes wind? Go to the library with your family and check out books on wind, air, weather, clouds and big windy storms like hurricanes and tornadoes. Check out books about the body and read all about the lungs—learn how you make wind each time you talk, breathe, blow up a balloon, or sing!

- What makes music? When you're at the library, see if you can find some books on what makes music and other sounds. Find out how chimes or bells make music by looking up "vibrations." Find out why you hear music from your Wind Chimes by looking up "ears" and "hearing."

- Go with your family on a Family Science Museum Outing! There are science museums and children's museums in many cities and towns. Many of them have exhibits on sound, vibrations, music, and hearing. Check them out!

- Many churches and schools have sets of bells. You and your family can attend a Bells Concert or Bell Choir performance and listen to the beautiful music of bells. Each bell makes a different note when it's rung, and when boys and girls ring different bells at different times, they make a song!

Rainbow Clothes

Tired of the same old T-shirt and blue jeans? Here's a way to decorate your wardrobe and get the whole family working together to give you a fresh new rainbow look!

What You'll Need for a Rainbow-riffic T-shirt:

- ➤ cotton T-shirt—a clean one!
- ➤ crayons
- ➤ paper
- ➤ clothes iron

Here's How to Make It:

1. Here's a great way to jazz up a plain T-shirt! First, draw a colorful crayon picture or design on a piece of paper. You can also draw directly onto a cotton T-shirt. Instead of a picture, you can print your name or a fun saying, write out your favorite sports team's name—whatever you'd like to write or draw. Be creative and colorful! Press hard on the crayons so you get lots of colorful waxy layers on your picture. Remember: if you draw or write on paper, it will be reversed when it's ironed into the T-shirt. It's best to write words directly onto the T-shirt rather than have to write backwards on paper!

2. Have a grownup help you with the ironing part. Set a clothes iron for the type of fabric you're using.

3. If you drew a picture on paper, place your drawing on the T-shirt with the crayon side down, directly on the cloth.

4. Have your grown-up helper slowly iron over your drawing. This heats up the crayon and works the colors into the cloth of your T-shirt. The colors will melt, get more colorful, and even spread out

72

a little on the cloth. If you drew on a paper, remove the paper and your Rainbow-riffic T-shirt is complete! If you drew directly onto the T-shirt, you're also done (if you got any crayon stuck onto the iron, have a grownup use a big wad of paper towel to wipe it off while the iron is still warm and it's easy to remove).

5. Your Rainbow-riffic T-shirt is safe for washing many times in cold or warm water without having the colors run or fade.

What You'll Need for a Tie-Dyed T-shirt:

➤ cotton T-shirt—a clean one!

➤ water

➤ food coloring or Color Magic dye (see page 59)

➤ eyedropper

➤ small bowls or cups— 1 for each color

➤ rubber bands or string

Here's How to Make It:

1. Pour some water into small cups or bowls, one container for each color you'd like to tie-dye with.

2. With an eyedropper, add drops of food coloring or Color Magic dye to the water and stir with a spoon. Add more drops until you get the color you want. Remember: mix red and yellow to make orange, mix blue and yellow to make green, and mix red and blue to make purple!

3. Now to prepare the T-shirt! All around the shirt, scrunch up the fabric into little balls and tie them off tightly with rubber bands or with string. One at a time, stick each ball of fabric into a container with the colored water and let it soak for a few minutes. Keep checking the fabric by lifting it out of the water until you think it's the right color. Carefully squeeze out any extra water from the fabric over the container or over a sink. Keep dipping the tied-off balls of fabric in colored water. You can make each tie-dyed area a different color or all the same color!

4. Another way to tie-dye (using one color only) is to fold up the shirt like an accordion and tightly tie four or five strings at different intervals across the rolled-up shirt. Place the entire shirt into a larger bowl of colored water and let it soak until you think it's the right color. Wring out extra water from the fabric over the container or over a sink.

5. Wash your tie-dyed shirt, still tied up, in the washing machine. Wash it separately from any other clothes! Use the regular amount of detergent and run it through a wash and rinse cycle. After the washing, take off the rubber bands or strings and air-dry your shirt. Then it's ready to wear!

More Family Fun:

Rainbow Clothes are fun to make and great to wear! If you get T-shirts in the right sizes, you can make Rainbow-riffic T-shirts and Tie-Dyed T-shirts for the whole family—it's a hot look, too! And there are many other things besides shirts that you can make with iron-ons and tie-dyes. All you need is some plain cloth or old sheets cut to the right size, and you can make some great gifts and other fun stuff:

- Wall hangings
- Flags
- Sewing projects
- Handkerchiefs
- Clubhouse signs
- Window curtains
- Placemats
- Sports banners
- Napkins
- Socks
- Puppet curtains
- Pillowcases

Papier-Mache Wonders

The craft magic of papier-mache, French for "chewed-up paper," recycles old newspapers and makes a wide variety of projects. This is one of the easiest family fun craft recipes!

What You'll Need:

- flour
- lukewarm water
- salt—just a pinch
- mixing spoon
- large mixing bowl
- old newspapers—
  torn into long strips,
  1–2 inches wide
- balloons—
  different shapes and sizes
- cardboard—boxes,
  tubes, etc.
- plastic bags
  or plastic wrap

- poster paints
- paintbrushes
- scissors

Here's How to Make It:

1 . Mix small amounts of flour and water in a large bowl to make a soupy paste. Keep adding more flour and water in the bowl, stirring as you go—you want a paste that's thin enough to coat the newspaper strips, but not watery enough to turn the newspaper into a soggy mess. When you have the right consistency, add a pinch of salt and stir it into the papier-mache paste.

2. Now prepare the forms for whatever you want to make! For example, if you want to make a traditional piñata (see "More Family Fun" on the next page), blow up different shapes of balloons to make an animal body, head, and legs. You can use other objects—try cardboard boxes and tubes, bowls, and jars—to make different shapes. Because you're going to dip strips of newspaper into the papier-mache paste and cover your form with them, you'll want to cover the form with a plastic bag or plastic wrap so the dried papier-mache will separate easily from the form. Don't bother to do that with balloons, though—all you do is POP them!

3. Dip long newspaper strips, cut one to two inches wide, into the papier-mache paste. What you want to do is lightly coat the strips, so after you dip them in the paste, use two fingers of one hand to squeeze extra paste off the strips. Then wrap the wet strips around your form. Crisscross the strips so that they overlap each other— that will make your creation strong.

4. Place your covered form on newspapers and set it aside to dry (it might take overnight to completely dry and harden). If you covered balloons, cut off their ends with scissors and remove the popped balloons from your hardened creation. If you used other forms, gently slide off the hardened papier-mache.

5. If you're making something a little more complicated, like an animal, you might need to connect your dried shapes with strips of fresh papier-mache. Use the strips of wet newspaper to overlap two or more forms (example: connect a larger round "body" to a smaller round "head" or a tube-shaped "trunk"). Set aside these forms until they are completely dry.

6. Decorate your project with poster paints.

More Family Fun:

Papier-mache makes a great family activity. You can get everyone together to mix the paste, dip the newspapers, prepare the forms, and cover the forms with wet strips—then there's the decorating! Here are some great ideas for projects:

● Make a piñata! This is a decorated animal or figure made out of papier-mache, filled with wrapped candies, treats, and coins. At Christmas time, birthdays or other parties, make a piñata and hang it from a tree branch or suspend it from the ceiling. One at a time, blindfold family members and friends and have them try to break open the piñata with a baseball bat. When the bat breaks open the papier-mache, everyone scrambles to collect the goodies that spill out!

● Make a scene on a piece of wood or cardboard. Use papier-mache to cover small juice boxes, shoeboxes, or other forms to make buildings. Use wet strips of paste-coated newspapers to attach your buildings to the wood or cardboard base, then paint your scene. Try making a scene of your neighborhood or a big map with papier-mache mountains, rivers, hills, valleys, and other scenes—ask your Mom or Dad to help you make a map of where you live.

● Make papier-mache sculptures or other original art forms!

● Make all kinds of masks and other costume pieces from papier-mache. You can make a mask using a large balloon or a gallon milk jug as a form. After the papier-mache dries, cut out eyes, mouth, and nose holes before decorating. Use a bowl as a form to make a helmet or other kind of hat. Use a piece of cardboard cut to the right shape to make a sword or other "props." Put on a play for your family and friends!

Solar System Mobile

Planets swirl through space every day, filling the sky with new worlds to explore. Bring that awesome wonder into your own room with this fun papier-mache mobile project!

What You'll Need:

- flour
- lukewarm water
- salt—just a pinch
- mixing spoon
- large mixing bowl
- old newspapers—torn into long strips, 1–2 inches wide
- balloons—round ones
- aluminum foil

- pipe cleaners or twist-ties
- cardboard or construction paper
- poster paints
- paintbrush
- string—10 pieces
- scissors
- dowel rod, yardstick, or wire coat hanger

Here's How to Make It:

1. First, prepare the forms for your Solar System Mobile! You'll need a grown-up helper to work with you to make spheres that will give you the nine planets of the solar system. Here is the order of the planets (moving outward from the sun) and how big around the forms should be: Mercury—3/8 inch; Venus—15/16 inch; Earth—1 inch; Mars—5/8 inch; Jupiter—11 inches; Saturn—10 inches; Uranus—4 inches; Neptune—4 inches; and Pluto—1/4 inch. For the big planets, blow up balloons to the right size. For the smaller planets, make forms by rolling up balls of aluminum foil.

2. Now for the papier-mache paste! Mix small amounts of flour and water in a large bowl to make a soupy paste. Keep adding more flour and water in the bowl, stirring as you go—you want a paste that's thin enough to coat the newspaper strips, but not watery enough to turn the newspaper into a soggy mess. When you have the right consistency, stir a pinch of salt into the paste.

3. Dip long newspaper strips, cut one to two inches wide, into the papier-mache paste. What you want to do is lightly coat the strips, so after you dip them in the paste, use two fingers of one hand to squeeze extra paste from the strips. Then wrap the wet strips around your different planet forms. Crisscross the strips so that they overlap each other—that will make your planets strong.

4. Add a pipe cleaner loop or a twist-tie loop at the top of each planet form—so you can hang them by strings when they're finished!

5. Place your covered forms on newspapers and set them aside to dry (it might take overnight to completely dry and harden). Once they've thoroughly dried, cut off the ends of the balloons with scissors and remove the popped balloons from your larger planets. Use fresh papier-mache strips to cover the hole where the balloon ends were. Set them aside to dry.

6. Decorate each of your nine papier-mache spheres with poster paints to make them look like the real planets! But first go to the library and check out a book on planets. Each planet has its own distinctive colors and surface patterns. Cut out cardboard or construction paper rings to fit around Saturn.

7. To complete your Solar System Mobile, tie different lengths of strings to the pipe cleaner or twist-tie loops at the top of each planet and attach the strings to a dowel rod or yardstick. Attach the planets in the order given in Step 1. Tie another string to the rod or yardstick and hang the mobile up—you may need to move the string off-center to make sure your mobile is properly balanced. An easy option is to tie your planets to a wire coat hanger—it even has its own handle for hanging! And there you are—a little bit of outer space right in your room!

More Family Fun:

Making the Solar System Mobile is a great family activity. You can get everyone together to mix the papier-mache paste, dip the news-papers, prepare the forms for each planet, and cover the forms with wet strips—then there's the decorating! Here are some ideas for other family projects:

● Make mobiles with other materials. Use papier-mache objects that you make, construction paper cutouts and shapes, found objects (like small or recycled items that you might find around your home), or other art materials to make mobiles. Experiment with different sizes and weights of objects, and even different dowel rods to create a delicately balanced mobile!

● Take a Family Star-Gazing Outing! Do you know anyone who has a telescope? If you do, that's wonderful, but you don't need one to take a night walk in a clear, open area (hopefully away from the city lights) and look up at the sky. What can you spot up there? Stars in different patterns (called constellations)? Planets? Airplanes? The moon?

● Take a trip to a planetarium, a place where they have special light shows about the planets, stars, and other heavenly bodies.

● Go to the library with your family and check out other books on outer space: astronomy, stars, galaxies, black holes, space travel, UFOs, and other great space topics!

Blender Paper

With a grown-up helper, you can make homemade paper in your kitchen. It's a great way to turn something old into something new—the power of recycling!

What You'll Need:

- ➤ blender
- ➤ lukewarm water
- ➤ old newspapers—torn into strips; newsprint only, not glossy or coated paper
- ➤ wire window screen—2 pieces
- ➤ aluminum foil

- ➤ scissors
- ➤ scotch tape
- ➤ plastic bag
- ➤ rolling pin
- ➤ dishtowel

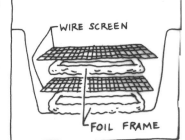

Here's How to Make It:

1. This is a grown-up step, but you can help! Start your Blender Paper recipe by tearing old newspapers into narrow strips (do not use the colorful, glossy-coated ad or magazine pages) . Fill the blender two-thirds full of lukewarm water. Have your grown-up helper turn the blender on the low setting, and then feed about ten newspaper strips into the swirling water. The Blender Paper recipe

84

is ready when the paper/water mixture is soupy and thick. Your grown-up helper should add more newspaper strips and blend well until the recipe is rich and thick enough.

2. Now make two frames for your Blender Paper. Each frame will have four sides for a square or a rectangular sheet of paper. Have your grown-up helper tear off four sheets of aluminum foil; each sheet should be about twelve inches long. Loosely roll up each foil sheet until it looks like a snake, then gently squeeze it so that the foil stays firmly rolled-up. These rolls of foil will be the sides of your paper-making frame, so decide how big you want your sheets of paper to be. Use scissors to cut the foil rolls to proper lengths for the sides. Tape the foil rolls together with a piece of tape at each corner. Now you have one frame! Have your helper tear off four more sheets of foil, roll them up, cut them to size, and tape them together to form the second frame. Both frames should be the same size!

3. Have your helper cut two pieces of wire window screen. The screen pieces should be the same size, and they should be cut so that they are larger than the aluminum foil frames you helped make in Step 2. Now put the frames and screens together in your kitchen sink: put one frame down on the bottom of your sink, lay a piece of screen over it, put the other frame on top of the screen (directly over the other frame), then lay the last screen on top.

4. Now you're ready to make Blender Paper! Pour the soupy paper gloop from the blender onto the top screen in your sink. Pour enough to cover the screen. Let the mixture drain through the screen. This might take five to ten minutes to let all the extra water drain into the sink.

5. After draining, take off the top screen (and the paper pulp on it) and put the screen and pulp on a counter or tabletop. Remove the top foil frame and take the second screen and lay it directly on the pulp and the other screen. Put a plastic bag over the screens and pulp and carefully roll the pulp flat and thin with a rolling pin. Remove the plastic bag and cover the screens and flattened pulp with a thick dishcloth. On top of the dishcloth place a heavy skillet, pan, or other weight. This will keep the Blender Paper flat while it dries.

6. Here's the hard part: you will have to wait one to three days for the paper to completely dry! To check if it's dry, take off the weight, lift up the towel, and touch the paper. If it is dry, carefully peel away the sheet of Blender Paper from the two screens. Use it like any sheet of paper—for cutting, coloring, drawing, or writing!

More Family Fun:

Because this recipe uses old newspapers to make new paper, this is a great recycling project. There are many fun family recycling projects you can help out with.

- Gather up old magazines, phone books, aluminum and glass containers, and newspapers for recycling—help a grown-up put them in containers for a recycling pickup.
- Visit a recycling center with your family and see where old things become new again!

And here are some more fun ideas for Blender Paper:

- Use cookie cutters to trace and cut out Blender Paper shapes. Use them for notes, letters, or invitations. Punch a hole in the top and add ribbon to hang paper ornaments up for holidays or special celebrations!
- Add color to your sheets of paper with drops of food coloring or Color Magic dye to the Blender Paper recipe!
- Before you use a rolling pin to flatten the paper pulp (in Step 5), sprinkle glitter on top of the paper to make it full of color and sparkles. You can also add strings of scrap fabric to decorate the paper.
- Punch holes in the side of several sheets of homemade paper and tie them together with yarn. Make your own booklet of drawings, stories, or family photographs. Then show them off to everyone!

Family Fun

Toys &
Playsets

Activity Book

Big Rhythm Band

Keep marching to the Big Beat with these Bongo Drums, Maracas, and Scrapers. Let the musical fun begin!

What You'll Need for Bongo Drums:

- ➤ empty two-pound coffee cans—1 or more (with plastic lids)
- ➤ unsharpened pencils—2
- ➤ construction paper
- ➤ crayons or markers
- ➤ scissors
- ➤ tape
- ➤ glitter, fabric scraps, feathers, or other art materials

Here's How to Make Them:

1. Use the eraser end of the two pencils as drumsticks. Drum on the plastic lids of the empty coffee cans to get a great bongo beat.

2. Make your bongo drums fancier by decorating construction paper with crayons, markers, glitter, or other craft materials. Tape the construction paper around the coffee cans to make your bongos beautiful!

3. You'll get a higher sound from an empty one-pound coffee can. Try making bongos from both one- and two-pound cans. Empty oatmeal containers, with the lids still on them, make a completely different sound. Tape different-sized "drums" together to make a bongo band!

What You'll Need for Maracas:

- ➤ empty fruit juice cans—2 or more (with lids)
- ➤ uncooked rice or dried beans
- ➤ construction paper
- ➤ crayons or markers
- ➤ scissors
- ➤ tape

Here's How to Make Them:

1. Real maracas look like rattles. You shake them to make music. Yours will look like decorated juice cans, but they will make the same great rhythm band music! Wash out two or more empty juice cans and dry them inside and out with a dishtowel. Wash and dry the lids, too.

2. Put a handful of uncooked rice or dried beans in each can.

3. Tape the lids tightly to the can. Use construction paper, crayons or markers, and other craft supplies to decorate the juice cans and lids. Just shake them to make mucho music!

4. For a quick set of maracas (which you should not decorate unless you check with a grownup), put different amounts of uncooked rice or dried beans in plastic food containers. If the lids do not tightly close onto the containers, tape them down. Here's a Music Hint: you'll get the best sound if you hold the containers sideways and shake them up and down.

*What You'll Need
for Scrapers:*

> ➤ scrap wood—2 pieces
> ➤ rough sandpaper—2 sheets
> ➤ scissors
> ➤ thumbtacks

Here's How to Make Them:

1. Cut the sandpaper sheets to fit around the scrap wood pieces. Attach the sandpaper sheets to the wood pieces with thumbtacks.

2. And you're already done! When you rub the wood blocks together, sandpaper against sandpaper, you'll make a rhythmic scraping sound.

More Family Fun:

Keep switching instruments with your family and friends so you can try out each one. Here are some more fun musical ideas:

- March to your own music
- Keep time to a record of favorite song
- Give your family and friends a concert
- Get your friends together for a Big Rhythm Band parade

Fast Track

Marbles are speedy, colorful wonderballs that you can send whizzing down your own raceway! Ping-pong balls are also fun to substitute for marbles (marbles are not safe toys for children under four years old).

What You'll Need:

➤ marbles or ping-pong balls
➤ paper towel tubes
➤ scissors
➤ construction paper
➤ crayons or markers
➤ tape or glue
➤ pillows
➤ books
➤ glitter, fabric scraps, feathers, or other art materials

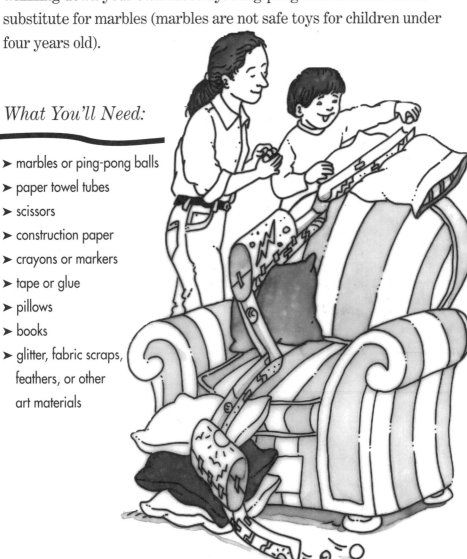

Here's How to Make It:

1. Cut the paper towel tubes in half lengthwise. Decorate the tubes with crayons or markers. Make lightning bolts, bright dots, stripes, or other designs. You can even use glue and glitter or other craft materials to decorate the tubes—the wilder, the better! Use construction paper and loop it around a tube if you'd like to make a tunnel.

2. Find a spot in the room that's higher than the floor, such as the top of a table or a bookshelf. Start building your Fast Track from this high point because you'll need the help of gravity to get your marbles moving! Use a pillow to provide support for the top of your track. Tape or glue the tubes together end to end. Overlap two tubes about one half inch for gluing or taping. Bend the last half inch of one tube before attaching another length of tube if you want to add an exciting drop-off to your track. Cut the end of one tube at an angle and attach another length of tube to add a little curve to your track. Use stacks of books or more pillows to add support to your track as it slopes down.

3. Keep taping or gluing tubes together so that your Fast Track slopes down to a chair. Use a pillow on the chair to support your track.

4. Keep taping or gluing tubes together—remember to add tunnels, curves, and drop-offs to your track for extra fun! Use a pillow or stack of books to support the track as you slope it down from the chair to the floor.

5. Now you're ready for some marble racing excitement! Drop a marble or ping-pong ball at the top of the Fast Track and let it roll, or start a whole handful of marbles and watch them race downhill.

6. Another way to set up a lightning-fast course is to start at the top of a flight of stairs and build your course down the stairs, from one landing to another. (But always be careful playing on stairs—it's best to play with a grownup nearby!)

More Family Fun:

● If you have enough paper towel rolls, try building two Fast Tracks, side-by-side. You can make them with different curves, tunnels, and drop-offs. Then race marbles or ping-pong balls down the two tracks.

● Try adding obstacles to your course. You can make holes in the bottom of some tubes to trap slower marbles. You can even split your track into two different sections. Just cut a slit in the middle of a tube, flatten out both halves, and tape or glue two tubes to the top of the halves. You can keep splitting your raceway into more tracks, or have the two tracks come together again!

● Friends and family members can have Fast Track races. Use a watch and see whose marble or ping-pong ball has the fastest run down the course. You can combine this racing idea with other racing activities for a Family Fun Race Night!

● Have you ever been to a race? Go with your family to a ski, track, or swim meet at a high school or college. Cheer on your favorite team of racers! Attend a horse or dog race. Or for ear-splitting fun, you and your family can go to a stock car or dragster race. It's even faster action than your Fast Track!

Go Fish!

You don't need a boat, a river, or a fancy rod and reel to go fishing. You don't even have to leave your house. Wow—this is one of the easiest ways you, your family, and your friends can go fishing!

What You'll Need:

- ➤ string—1 or more pieces, 2–3 feet long
- ➤ scissors
- ➤ masking tape
- ➤ yardstick, giftwrap paper tube, or large stick
- ➤ large paper clips
- ➤ old magazines
- ➤ construction paper
- ➤ crayons or markers
- ➤ small horseshoe magnet— 1 or more
- ➤ large cardboard box

Here's How to Make It:

1. Find something around the house that you can use for a fishing pole—a yardstick, a paper tube from some giftwrap, or a large stick works fine.

2. To make your "fishing line," cut a piece of string 2–3 feet long and tape it to one end of your fishing pole.

3. Tie a small horseshoe magnet to the end of your fishing line. You can use any kind of magnet that is easy to tie onto your line.

4. Now, make some fish! You can find pictures of fish in old sporting magazines and cut them out. You can also draw pictures of fish on construction paper. Color them with crayons or markers and cut them out. Attach a large metal paper clip near the mouth of each fish. (Be careful with paper clips—they're easy to swallow for children under four years old!)

5. Set up your "fishing hole" by scattering your fish on the floor. Sit in a chair or on a sofa—that's your boat—and use the magnet on your pole to "hook" a fish. The paper clips on the fish will be attracted to the magnet and you'll be able to pull in those big ones!

6. For even more fishing fun, decorate a big cardboard box to look like a boat. Scatter your fish on the floor, hop in your boat box, and go fish!

More Family Fun:

● Make a fun Go Fish Game! On the back of each fish, draw a big number—make all the numbers different. Scatter the fish all around the floor, number side down, and go fishing. Each player gets two turns and can catch two fish. Add the numbers on the back of each fish. The player with the highest point total is the winner. For more of a challenge, make sure you can't see the fish. Scatter them inside a cardboard box, behind a sofa, or around a bed. Or try using a blindfold—no peeking!

● Use pipe cleaners or twist-ties instead of magnets and paper clips. Bend a pipe cleaner or twist-tie into a hook shape and tie it to your fishing string. Cut out fish from old magazines or construction paper, then paste them to a piece of cardboard. Cut out your cardboard fish. Punch a hole near the mouth of each fish. Loop a pipe cleaner or twist-tie through the hole and make it into a circle. Now try to "hook" your fish!

● Make a wet Go Fish game. Cut out fish from foam trays (from many fast food restaurants), attach paper clips, and float your fish in a bathtub or sink. Or go outside and float them in a big tub or wading pool. Add numbers to the back sides of the fish to play the Go Fish Game!

● Learn all about fishing from the library! Check out books about different kinds of fish, as well as fishing stories and books about the sport of fishing.

● Go with your family to a pet store or an aquarium to learn more about real fish! Maybe you can even set up your own fishbowl or home aquarium and learn how to take care of pet fish.

● Go on a Family Fishing Outing—you can make a great weekend trip out of fishing, or just spend a fun afternoon together! Most cities and towns have rivers, lakes, streams, or ponds for fishing. Many sporting goods stores, bait shops, or resorts will rent fishing rods, reels, and tackle. Take a picnic lunch and fish from shore or rent a boat. Have a grownup show you how to bait a hook, cast it into the water, play with the line, reel in a fish, and take it off the hook. And if you're camping out, learn how to clean and cook what you catch!

Potato Face Family

Potato heads have been fun for boys and girls—practically forever! It's a creative family project that gives lots of belly laughs when the potato faces turn out to be quite silly.

What You'll Need:

- ➤ large baking potatoes—
  1 or more
- ➤ vegetable scrub brush
- ➤ clay, play dough, or Quick Play
  Clay (see page 5)
- ➤ toothpicks

- ➤ construction paper
- ➤ felt, ribbons, bows, and other
  craft materials
- ➤ scissors
- ➤ crayons or markers

Here's How to Make Them:

1. Clean one or more large baking potatoes with a vegetable scrub brush. Dry the potatoes thoroughly.

2. Now you can make different facial features for your Potato Face people! Use clay, play dough, or Quick Play Clay to make a nose, eyes, mouth, and ears. Felt, construction paper, and other craft materials also make great features if you don't have clay. Felt makes a great beard and mustache. You can use tassles, yarn, and other craft materials for hair.

3. A grown-up helper can cut toothpicks in half. Use these to stick features on your Potato Face—they're especially good for sticking on the clay items. If you're using Quick Play Clay, insert the cut-off end of the toothpick half into the back of your clay nose, eyes, mouth, or ears. That leaves the sharp end sticking out, ready to insert into your Potato Face. You can bake the Quick Play Clay features in the oven, then paint them when they're hard!

104

4. Make a clay base for your Potato Face to sit upright on. Press the bottom of the potato into some clay and mold the clay snugly around the bottom. You can model the clay to make a shirt collar, bowtie, or add a real bow or ribbon!

5. Use different sizes of potatoes to make an entire Potato Face family. Mix and match the facial features, hair, hats, and other decorations to make your Potato Faces scary, silly, or beautiful!

More Family Fun:

- Every member of the family can create a Potato Face. It's fun to see what everyone makes!
- After you've had a chance to play potato dress-up, have a grownup make delicious baked potatoes. Choose toppings for your hot potatoes—melted cheese, cooked veggies, chili, sour cream, or melted butter are good picks.

● If you don't want to eat your Potato Face friends, you can make a Potato Print! Have a grownup cut your potato lengthwise. Then draw a simple picture or design on a potato half with a black felt pen. Your grown-up helper can use a paring or X-acto knife to cut away the potato around what you drew, cutting back about 1/4 inch all around your art. Then pour some poster or tempera paint into a shallow dish or saucer. Gently dip your potato into the paint. Stamp out a picture of your art onto a piece of paper. You can also make a multi-colored print—with a paintbrush, dab different colors onto your potato stamp before you press it on the paper! Experiment with different potato designs, letters of the alphabet, and numbers. You need to draw letters and numbers backwards so they will read correctly when you stamp them—a grownup can help you with this backwards writing.

Wet and Wild

Ahoy, mates! Get ready to set sail for the high seas, adventure, and fun family times with your own fleet of rafts, sailboats, and speedboats.

What You'll Need:

- popsicle or craft sticks—12
- glue
- plastic container or paper cup
- toothpicks
- construction paper
- scissors
- crayons or markers
- tape
- empty milk or juice carton— half gallon size
- large balloon

107

Here's How to Make Them:

1. To make a raft, glue eight clean popscicle or craft sticks side-by-side. Glue one stick across each of the four ends to strengthen the raft. Now you have a floating toy. Put it in a pool, sink, or bathtub and float some toys on it!

2. To make a sailboat, cut out a triangle from a piece of construction paper. Decorate it with crayons or markers. Now you have a sail—glue it to a toothpick and tape it to the side of a plastic container. Anchors away!

3. To make a speedboat, slice a half gallon milk or juice carton in half lengthwise. Each half will be a boat. Use tape or glue to make sure all parts of each boat are sealed tight. Next, cut a small 3/8 inch hole in the back end of the boat. Put a large balloon inside the open boat and push the end of the balloon through the hole. Have a grownup help you blow up the balloon. Hold the end shut and place your speedboat in water. Let go of the balloon, and watch your craft z-o-o-m!

More Family Fun:

It's fun to play in the water. If you're taking a bath, sail your craft around dangerous mountains of soapsuds. In the swimming pool, sail your craft from one side of the pool to the other. Here are some more Wet and Wild ideas:

● Set up a Floating Game for your rafts and boats. Cut out different shapes from foam trays (found in many fast food restaurants). Use a marker and put a number on each shape and float them in the sink, tub, or pool. Blow your raft or sailboat towards each shape—touch one to win points! Each player gets a certain amount of time to sail for the most points.

● Have races with your balloon-powered speedboat. Your family and friends will have fun sailing boats from one side of the tub or pool to the other!

● Take your watercraft on a Family Beach Outing! Build sand castles and a boat launch area for your craft. Make a small lake for your raft and boats. Take a picnic lunch, a frisbee, and lots of sand toys, too.

● Take a boat ride with your family. Rent a canoe, a paddleboat, a speedboat, a sailboat, a ferryboat, a fishing boat, a rubber raft, or even a floating tube to have some fun on the water!

● Check out all the Wet and Wild action at a water theme park!

● Check out books on boats, ships, rafts, and sailboats from the library!

Puffy Blocks

They're big! They're stackable! They're fun to play with! ...and they're puffy! You'll enjoy making these paper bag blocks, and you and your friends will have hours of fun playing with them.

What You'll Need:

> ➤ large grocery bags—10 or more
> ➤ crayons or markers
> ➤ old newspapers
> ➤ masking tape

Here's How to Make Them:

1. If you'd like, take crayons or markers and decorate both sides of large grocery bags before you make them into blocks. It isn't something you have to do, but it's fun!

2. Lay a bag flat on a table or other work surface. Fold the top of the bag over about three inches, then crease the bag along the fold you just made.

3. Open the grocery bag completely.

4. Crumple up twelve sheets of old newspaper and stuff the wads of paper into the grocery bag.

110

5. Fold the bag shut on the crease lines you made in Step 2 above. Use masking tape to seal the bag shut. (Packing tape is extra wide and also does a good job of sealing the bags.)

6. Make ten or more of these great Puffy Blocks and you're ready for some big building action! They're fun to stack up, and they're fun and safe to knock down, too.

7. If your blocks rip, repair them with tape or make a new block. If they get wet or just a little damp, you can leave them in the sun or in a warm room to dry and they will be as good as new again!

More Family Fun:

● Decorate your Puffy Blocks to look like different building materials:

    —logs, to make a log cabin

    —bricks, to build a pretty house
      (make some windows and a door, too)

    —stone, to build a castle (don't forget to decorate
      some blocks to look like towers, windows,
      and a drawbridge!)

● Make a Puffy Blocks Bowling Game! Stack up four or more blocks on top of each other to form a giant bowling pin. Make stacks of other blocks, too, and line them up beside each other. Stand back and roll a ball towards the "pins" to see who can knock down the most blocks!

● Add cardboard boxes, clotheslines and blankets, and other items to your Puffy Blocks building fun! Make ramps, towers, bridges, roofs, etc.

● Now that you're in the construction business, go on a Family Building Outing! Visit an office, store, or home construction site and have a grownup arrange for you and your family to take a tour.

Trains 'n' Planes

Don't throw those large empty boxes away! Turn them into great vehicles that let your imagination run wild. Your whole family will have fun turning cardboard into something completely new.

What You'll Need:

- large cardboard boxes— 1 or more
- paper towel tubes—1 or more
- plastic containers—1 or more; yogurt containers work well
- paper plates—4 or more
- tape, paste, or glue

- construction paper
- crayons or markers
- scissors

Here's How to Make Them:

1. Cut off or push up the bottom and top flaps of a big cardboard box. Now you can stand inside the box!

2. To make a train, add wheels to both sides of the box. Draw wheels with crayons or markers. You can also cut wheels out of construction paper or color some paper plates to look like wheels, then tape or glue them to the box.

3. Tape a paper towel tube to the inside of the front part of your box for a smokestack. Tape a plastic container to the front for a headlight. Draw a cowcatcher under the headlight.

4. To make a plane, draw round pretend windows with people in them and add them to both sides of the box. Use crayons, markers, or construction paper.

5. Now add airplane wings and a headlight! Remove the bottom and top from the cardboard box. Then cut out two wing shapes from the extra cardboard. Decorate them with crayons, markers, or construction paper. Put a one-inch fold at the end of each wing, then tape them to the sides of the box. Tape a plastic container to the front for a headlight.

6. Now you're ready to play with your train or plane. Imagine you, your family, and your friends are a long train with many cars. Or pretend you're flying high in the sky—go right through the clouds!

More Family Fun:

Have your friends or other family members each make something different—then you can have a parade around the house or neighborhood. To make your vehicles more true-to-life, go to the library and check out some vehicle books. Customize your cardboard box creations with colors and lettering from the trains and planes you read about. Here are some more great things you can make with boxes:

- A Big-Wheel Truck
- A Sailboat
- A Rocket Ship
- A Flying Saucer
- A School Bus
- A Circus Car
- An Ocean Liner
- A Race Car
- A Tractor
- A Subway Car
- A Parade Float—Cover your box with colored tissue paper.
- A Shoebox Train Pull-Toy—Use shoeboxes to make a small train. Connect the shoebox cars with string and pull them along the floor!

Sky Movers

Take two chairs, a length of string, and a little imagination to make an aerial cable car, sky tram, rocket ship, or jet racer!

What You'll Need:

- ➤ toilet paper or paper towel tubes—1 or more
- ➤ plastic drinking straw
- ➤ play dough—a small piece
- ➤ tape, paste, or glue
- ➤ construction paper
- ➤ crayons or markers

- ➤ string—1 or 2 pieces, 6–10 feet long or enough to go across a room
- ➤ scissors
- ➤ chairs—2, 4, or more
- ➤ large balloons

Here's How to Make Them:

1. To make a short Sky Mover, use a toilet paper tube. Use a paper towel tube for a longer Sky Mover. Tape or glue a two-inch piece of plastic drinking straw lengthwise along the outside of the toilet paper tube, right in the center. For a paper towel tube, use a four-inch piece of straw.

2. Decorate your Sky Mover with crayons or markers. Turn the tube into a sky tram or cable car by drawing windows and people. Use construction paper to make wings for a jet racer. Tape or glue them to the sides of the tube. Make construction paper fins and turn the tube into a rocket!

3. Have a grown-up helper cut a piece of string six to ten feet long. Feed the string through the straw on your Sky Mover, then tie each end of the string to a different chair. One end of the string should be higher than the other end—that's important! Place the two chairs apart so the string is pulled tight.

4. Now for a step that will help your Sky Mover actually move. Press a little piece of play dough inside the tube or tape a small toy inside the tube and pretend your Sky Mover is transporting an animal, a car, or another object through the air!

5. Slide your Sky Mover to the high end of the string, then let it slide to the low end by itself. Your Sky Mover is zooming through the air—you did it!

6. Tie a second piece of string to your two chairs and make another Sky Mover. Now you can race them! Add more strings, more chairs, and more Sky Movers for a really big race.

More Family Fun:

● Here's another Sky Mover idea. Tape a two-inch piece of drinking straw to the side of a large balloon and feed a string through the straw. Blow up the balloon, pinch the end shut, then let go to send your balloon shooting across the string skyway! Add more strings and chairs for a big Sky Mover balloon race.

● Try stringing balloon-powered Sky Movers on very long pieces of string and setting chairs at opposite ends of the room for a longer race. Keep blowing up the balloons when they deflate, and see who can get to the other side of the room first!

● Have you ever ridden in an aerial cable car or sky tram? Have you ever flown in an airplane? Visit the library with friends or family and check out books on these real-life sky movers. Use pictures of real vehicles to give you ideas for decorating your toy Sky Movers.

● Here's another great family fun idea: visit an airport and take a tour!

118

Rocket Power

Zoom, zoom, zoom to the moon in your balloon-powered spacecraft— buckle in, get ready for the countdown, then blast off!

What You'll Need:

➤ skinny, long balloons—1 or more
➤ plastic drinking straw
➤ rubber band

➤ old postcards—1 or more
➤ scissors
➤ pencil

Here's How to Make It:

1. With scissors, cut a plastic drinking straw in half. Slightly pinch in one end of one of the straw halves and slide it inside the other straw half. Completely insert the one inside the other. This gives you a heavier, stronger base for your rocket!

2. Insert the double straw a few inches into the opening of a long, skinny balloon. Make sure you use only straight balloons, not the round kind.

3. Wrap a rubber band around the neck of the balloon so it forms a tight seal around the straw.

4. Cut a small one inch by three inch rectangle from an old post-card. Fold it in half and cut a small notch along the fold. Slip the straw through the notch so that the postcard just clears the end of the straw. The postcard should fit snugly on the straw. If it's loose, you can secure it with a little piece of tape. Now your rocket has a stabilizer fin!

5. "Rocket to Mission Control, we are ready for launching!" Blow up the balloon by blowing through the straw. Keep the air from leaking out by pinching the straw shut or holding a finger over it.

6. Tilt your rocket balloon at a slight angle and take your fingers away from the straw. "Mission Control, we have liftoff!"

120

7. Experiment with your rocket. If it just spins around like a regular balloon, that means the stabilizer fin is too small. Cut out a bigger rectangle from another postcard and try that. You can also pinch the straw tighter at the end to allow less air to escape before you let go. Or you can poke the straw with a pencil or large nail to make the hole larger if you need more thrusting power.

More Family Fun:

● Here's another Rocket Power idea. See how high you can send your balloon rocket by aiming it straight up into the air.

● Try racing your balloon rocket with another friend's rocket! Who can cross the finish line first? Who can send his or her rocket the highest?

● Set up a rocket target. Have a contest with your family and friends and see whose rocket lands closest to the target area (like a cardboard box or a chalk circle drawn on the sidewalk).

● Go to the library and check out books on space stations, Cape Canaveral, historic rocket launches, and what makes rockets work! If you're lucky, you can watch a rocket launch on TV—they're very exciting!

Flying Fun

I t's amazing what you can do with paper and a few other items. You can make projects that fly, float, and spin through the air!

What You'll Need:

- ➤ paper—1 or more sheets of regular notebook paper
- ➤ tape
- ➤ large paper clip
- ➤ scissors
- ➤ handkerchief or square piece of fabric

- ➤ string—5 pieces, 4 inches long
- ➤ pipe cleaner or twist-tie
- ➤ small toy—very lightweight
- ➤ crayons, markers, or water-based fabric paint

Here's How to Make Them:

1. To make a paper airplane, fold a piece of paper in half. Then fold down the corners as shown in the picture (A). Fold the paper in half again (B). Then fold each side down to the center point (C). When you fold down the two sides, you form the wings of your

122

airplane (D). Put a small piece of tape across the wings to hold your plane together. Decorate your plane with crayons or markers and it's ready to fly!

2. To make a paper helicopter, have a grown-up helper cut a piece of paper into a rectangle two inches by eight and a half inches. Follow the picture and make the three cuts shown with a scissors. Cut #1 will be the helicopter blades. When you make that cut, fold the blades in opposite directions at the fold line. Cuts #2 and #3 will help you fold the bottom of your helicopter into thirds, as shown. When you have the folding done, fold up the bottom about one half inch and use a large paper clip to hold it in place. Color the blades with crayons or markers. When you drop the helicopter, watch it twirl to the ground!

3. To make a parachute, start with a handkerchief or square piece of fabric. Decorate the fabric with markers or fabric paint (found at most craft supply stores). Have a grownup help you tie a piece of string, cut to exactly four inches in length, to each of the four corners of your cloth. Tie the loose ends of the strings to a small loop you've made from a pipe cleaner or a twist-tie. Cut another short length of string, tie it to the bottom of the loop, and tie a small lightweight toy to the other end (like a small animal toy or doll). Drop the parachute from a high spot—like a stairwell or on top of a chair—or throw it up in the air and watch it float to the ground!

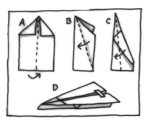
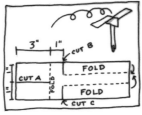

More Family Fun:

- Visit the library and check out books on aircraft and the sport of parachute jumping (skydiving). Use pictures of real planes and helicopters to decorate your paper creations.
- Have a Family Flight Outing and visit an airport—or take a helicopter ride if you can find one that's open to the public. Don't forget to take a camera and snap lots of pictures!

Your family and friends will enjoy playing with your Flying Fun airplane, helicopter, and parachute. Here are some more Flying Fun ideas:

- Have a contest to see who has the longest paper airplane flight!
- Set up a target on the ground with chalk or using an object such as a small box. Drop your paper helicopter or parachute and see who can come closest to the target!
- Tie a small box to the bottom of your parachute and make a parachute ride. Put different small toys in the box and give them a ride! Try light toys and heavier toys to see how they float differently.

What a Card!

Take an old deck of playing cards and make something special.
With a pair of scissors, you can turn them into building blocks!

What You'll Need:

➤ old deck of playing cards or index cards

➤ scissors

➤ crayons or markers

Here's How to Make Them:

1. First, take an old playing card or an index card (three inch by five inch cards work best) and a pair of scissors. Now get ready to make six cuts or notches in the card.

2. Cut two notches one half inch long into one of the long sides of the card. Make the cuts an inch from each end.

3. Cut two more notches one half inch long into the opposite long side of the card, an inch from each end. Make sure your notches line up across from each other on both sides!

4. Cut one notch one half inch long into one of the short ends of the card, right in the center.

5. Cut one more notch one half inch long into the opposite short end of the card, in the center. Make sure your notches line up across from each other on both ends!

6. Continue Steps 2–4 on other playing cards or index cards. The more cards you notch, the more you'll be able to build!

7. If you are using index cards, decorate both sides with crayons or markers. Make your Building Cards different colors. Draw different designs. Make them look like building materials: bricks, stone blocks, logs, windows, doors, pretty colored panels. Use your imagination!

8. Now you're ready to build. Slide Building Cards together at an angle by lining up the notches in the cards. Fit them together snugly. There are a zillion ways you can put the cards together to form walls, towers, buildings, robots, planes, cars—practically anything!

More Family Fun:

● Make a Building Cards Skyscraper! Lay a flat piece of cardboard or posterboard on top of a level of your Building Cards. Now add another level of Building Card walls. Place another piece of cardboard or posterboard on top of this level. Keep building levels. How high can you go?

● Go with your family to the library and check out books on how buildings are built! There are also great books on how pyramids, castles, and other famous structures were made and what's inside of them. Can you make buildings like those with your Building Cards?

● Play a card game! If your Building Cards are made from an old deck of playing cards, then here's how to play Have a Heart: Three or more players sit in a circle on the floor. Shuffle the cards and deal all of them out to each player. Cards are laid face down in front of players. Play begins to the left of the dealer. The first player flips over his or her first card in the pile and quickly puts it down in the center of the circle. Each player keeps flipping over a card and putting it down on the pile in the center of the circle. If at any time a Heart card is turned over, the player who has the Heart gets to take the whole pile and add it to his or her hand! Continue playing until one player takes all the cards.

● Here's how to play Gotcha, another great card game! Three or more players sit in a circle on the floor. Shuffle the cards and deal all of them out to each player. Players hold their cards in their hands and sort them by suit. Also sort them by value, with Ace counting as one, number cards from two to ten counting their face value, then Jack, Queen, and King (the highest card). Play begins to the left of the dealer. The first player lays down any card and says, "Eenie." Any player with the next card of higher value—in the same suit, too—lays down that card and says, "Meenie." The next higher card is laid down and that player says, "Minie." Then the fourth card is laid down and that player says, "Moe." The player with the fifth card completes the grouping by yelling, "Gotcha!" The cards are removed from play and the "Gotcha!" player starts a new group by laying down any card. Anytime a King, the highest card value, is played, then the group ends and that King is a "Gotcha!" Also, if the higher cards in any group have already been played, the last card that can be played is a "Gotcha!" The first player who runs out of cards is the winner.

Grown-Up Places

The world is filled with grown-up stuff, like stores, banks, offices, post offices, and factories. Now you can make your own Grown-Up Places!

What You'll Need:

- large cardboard boxes—3
- small cardboard box—1
- shoe box, with lid—1
- paper towel or toilet paper tubes—1 or more
- plastic lids—1 or more; yogurt container tops work well
- brads or metal fasteners—1 or more (available at stationery supply stores)
- tape, paste, or glue
- construction paper
- crayons or markers
- art materials
- scissors
- play money
- junk mail
- toy telephone

Here's How to Make Them:

1. To make a store or a bank, you'll need one large cardboard box. Have a grown-up helper cut the top off the box to let in light. Cut a door in the back of the box so you can get inside the store—or the bank teller's work space! Cut a window in the front of the box and use the extra cardboard to make a little ledge to tape to the bottom of the window. Use this ledge for the play money that you'll be collecting from people who want to buy things in your store or put money in your bank. If you want to make a grocery store, collect empty cereal boxes, milk containers, juice cans, and other used containers. Decorate your store or bank with crayons, markers, construction paper, and other art materials—and don't forget to make a sign!

2. To make a factory machine, you'll need one large cardboard box. Tape the box closed. Tape paper towel or toilet paper tubes to the top of the box for smokestacks. Have a grown-up helper cut a small hole in the back so you can place toys or other items into your machine. Cut a small flap in the front of the box, a flap you can lift up to take out the things your machine makes! Make a handle out of cardboard and tape it to the flap. Now, decorate your machine with crayons, markers, construction paper, or other art materials. Draw dials, buttons, pipes, and lots of machinery thing-a-majigs on all sides of the box. Have a grown-up helper stick brads or metal fasteners through the center of plastic lids and attach them to your machine. Push out the metal ends of the brads to secure the lids—now you have dials you can really turn! Cut out construction paper circles and tape or glue them to the lids. Attach one or more paper towel tubes to the sides of the box with brads or metal fasteners—now you have levers you can really pull!

3. To make an office, you'll need one small cardboard box and one shoebox with a lid. Tape the small box closed. Draw a computer screen on the front of the box with crayons or markers, or cut one out of construction paper and tape or paste it to the box. Have a grown-up helper cut a slot in the box for your "computer disks." Cut out pretend computer disks from pieces of construction paper. Use the shoebox lid for your keyboard—make "keys" out of construction paper and tape or glue them to the lid. Use the shoebox for your "In" basket and fill it with junk mail—you will need to open these up in your busy office! Add a toy telephone, and your office is ready. Set up your computer and other office supplies on a table or desk, and you're in business!

4. To make a post office, you'll need one large cardboard box. Tape the box closed. Near the top of the box, have a grown-up helper cut a flap that bends towards you—that's the slot where you put your mail in the mailbox! Make a handle out of cardboard and tape it to the mail slot. Draw the word "MAIL" on the slot, too! Cut another flap at the bottom of the box so you can pick up all the mail that's been put in the box. Decorate your mailbox using crayons, markers, or other art materials. Use junk mail and old envelopes around the house to play post office with. You can also cut out stamps and other pieces of mail from construction paper. Set your mailbox near a desk or table and have friends and family drop in some mail for you to deliver!

More Family Fun:

● Have your friends make their own stores and banks, factory machines, offices, and post offices. Put them all together and have a real Grown-Up Places town!

● Go on family errands to these real grown-up places! Maybe someone in your family works in one of these places—see if you can visit him or her at their job.

● Take a factory tour with your family! See how things are made, put together, packaged, and shipped.

● Go to the library and check out books on grown-up work places. Learn all about the work grownups do. What would you like to be when you grow up? Talk it over with your family!

Big Star TV & Radio

There are many famous people who act, read the news and weather, and perform music on TV and radio. Now you can make a giant TV or radio, make up your own shows and acts, and pretend to be a famous star!

What You'll Need:

- ➤ large cardboard boxes—2
- ➤ paper towel tubes—3
- ➤ plastic lids—4 or more; yogurt container tops work well
- ➤ brads or metal fasteners— 4 or more (available at stationery supply stores)

- ➤ tape, paste, or glue
- ➤ construction paper
- ➤ crayons or markers
- ➤ art materials—glitter, white liquid glue, fabric pieces, etc.
- ➤ scissors

Here's How to Make Them:

1. To make a Big Star TV, you'll need one large cardboard box. Tape the box closed.

2. Cut the bottoms of two paper towel tubes at an angle and tape them in a "V" shape to the top of the box for TV antennae.

3. Have a grown-up helper cut a small door in the back of the box so you can get inside the TV. Your helper can also cut a big window in the front of the box for your TV screen.

4. Decorate your TV with crayons, markers, construction paper, and other art materials. Put a big glittery star over the TV screen, because this is a Big Star TV!

5. Don't forget to make dials so you can have your family and friends change channels! Have a grown-up helper stick brads or metal fasteners through the center of plastic lids and attach them to your TV, just below the screen. Push out the metal ends of the brads to secure the lids—now you have dials you can really turn! Cut out construction paper circles and tape or glue them to the lids.

6. To make a Big Star Radio, you'll need one large cardboard box. Tape the box closed.

7. Tape a paper towel tube to the top of the box for a radio antenna.

8. Have a grown-up helper cut a small door in the back of the box so you can get inside the radio. Cut small windows in each side to let in light.

9. Decorate your radio with crayons, markers, construction paper, and other art materials. Draw a speaker grille on the front of the box with crayons or markers. Other speaker options: you can tape or glue pieces of construction paper to form a speaker or cut a big rectangle of fabric and glue it on the box. Put a big glittery star over the speaker grille, because this is a Big Star Radio!

10. Don't forget to make dials so you can have your family and friends change channels! Have a grown-up helper stick brads or metal fasteners through the center of plastic lids and attach them to your radio, just below the speaker. Push out the metal ends of the brads to secure the lids. Cut out construction paper circles and tape or glue them to the lids—now get ready to turn those dials to your favorite station!

More Family Fun:

● Invite your family and friends to sit in front of your Big Star TV or Radio and enjoy a special show! Here are some great ideas for shows: sing your favorite songs, read stories and poems, give a weather report, make up commercials for your toys or other products, or tell news about what you did today or news about your family, school and friends.

● Use your Big Star TV to put on a puppet show for your family and friends! Decorate a piece of shelf paper and tape it to the inside back of the TV box for a colorful background.

● Go to the library and check out books on TV and radio. How do they work? You can also find books about your favorite singers, actors, and other Big Stars!

● Go on a Family Big Star Outing! Tour a TV or radio station and see all the behind-the-scenes work that goes into putting on a program. Maybe you and your family can visit the set of a TV show and sit in the audience. See if you can get the autograph of a TV performer or radio disc jockey!

● Talk with your family about good ways to watch and listen to TV and radio around your home. Discuss which times are good TV and radio times and which times are good for quiet time, reading books, making things, and playing games. If you want to watch TV, try to choose one favorite show to watch each day. There are lots of good shows to pick from, like animal and nature programs, kids' specials, sports events, etc. And remember: watching too much TV takes away from all the fun you could be having with your family and friends!

Yummy Land

Food, food, food—everybody loves tasty treats and good meals, so let's take a trip to Yummy Land and make a pizza kitchen and an ice cream cart!

What You'll Need:

- medium cardboard boxes—2
- empty pizza delivery box
- paper towel tubes—2 or more
- popsicle or craft sticks— 2 or more
- toilet paper tubes—1 or more
- plastic lids—1 or more; yogurt container tops work well
- paper plates—4
- brads or metal fasteners— 5 or more (available at stationery supply stores)

- play dough or Hotstuff Play Clay (see page 28)—different colors
- tape, paste, or glue
- construction paper
- crayons or markers
- art materials
- scissors
- rolling pin
- cookie sheet
- food grater or garlic press
- play money
- toy telephone

Here's How to Make Them:

1. To make a pizza kitchen, you'll need one medium-sized cardboard box. Tape the box closed. Have a grown-up helper cut a flap in the front of the box, a flap you can pull down and open for

138

baking your pizza in this special pizza oven! Make a handle out of cardboard and tape it to the flap. Have a grown-up helper stick brads or metal fasteners through the center of plastic lids and attach them above the pizza oven door. Push out the metal ends of the brads to secure the lids—now you have cooking dials you can really turn! Cut out construction paper circles and tape or glue them to the lids. Now, decorate your oven with crayons, markers, construction paper, or other art materials.

2. To make a fresh, tasty, pretend pizza, take a large ball of play dough or Hotstuff Play Clay and use a rolling pin to roll it flat into a large circle. Put it on a cookie sheet. Make your favorite play dough toppings and put them on top of the pizza base: small red play dough circles (pepperoni), small chunks of brown play dough (hamburger), and shreds of yellow play dough that you've put through a food

139

grater or garlic press (cheese). Put the cookie sheet and pretend pizza into your pizza oven, close the flap, turn the dials, and wait for the pizza to cook!

3. When the pizza is "ready," take it out of the oven and slide it from the cookie sheet into an empty pizza delivery box. Take pizza orders on a toy phone and have family and friends help you make pizza deliveries and buy pizza with play money. Maybe you can help cut up the pizza and have a pretend pizza party!

4. To make an ice cream cart, you'll need one medium-sized cardboard box. Tape the box closed. Have a grown-up helper cut a flap in the top of the box, a flap you can pull open to take out special ice cream treats! Make a handle out of cardboard and tape it to the flap. Have a grown-up helper stick brads or metal fasteners through the center of paper plates and attach two on each side of the box, near the bottom—these are your ice cream cart wheels. Push out the metal ends of the brads to secure the plates. Now they really turn! Attach one paper towel tube to the side of the box with two brads or metal fasteners—this is the handle you use to push your cart. Decorate the wheels and the rest of the cart using crayons, markers, construction paper, or other art materials.

5. Make pretend ice cream treats. To make pretend popsicles or ice cream bars, tape or glue popsicle or craft sticks inside toilet paper tubes. Using crayons or markers, color the tubes brown for ice cream bars and different bright colors for popsicles. Use toilet paper tubes for ice cream cones. Color them brown with crayons or markers. To make pretend ice cream, wad up a piece of colored construction paper into a ball and tape it to the top of the tube. Now the ice cream cart can make its deliveries to families up and down the block. Hmmmm—it's so tasty here in Yummy Land!

More Family Fun:

• Have your friends help you play with your Yummy Land pizza kitchen and ice cream cart! They can add these to the Grown-Up Places store and bank, factory machine, office, and post office (see page 129). Put them all together and have a real Grown-Up Places and Yummy Land town!

• Go on a Family Pizza Party Outing! Celebrate a birthday, holiday, or just a fun dinner together at a pizza restaurant. Order your favorite toppings and share that good-tasting food with everyone. Perhaps a grownup can arrange for you to take a tour of the kitchen—see the pizza oven and meet the people who make the dough, sauce, and toppings!

● Take an ice cream factory tour with your family! If you have an ice cream plant or dairy products center in your town, see how ice cream, milk and other dairy treats are made, packaged and shipped.

● Go to the library and check out books on pizzas, restaurants, ice cream, and dairy products. These books might even have recipes that you and your family can use to make your own treats.

● Have a Family Do-It-Yourself Pizza and Ice Cream Sundae Party! Make mini-pizza crusts and have each member of your family pour on sauce and add his or her own favorite pizza toppings. Set up a make-your-own-sundae counter complete with ice cream, chocolate and other flavored syrups, crushed nuts, sprinkles, cherries, bananas, whipped cream, and other goodies.

Family Fun

Action
Games

Activity Book

Stuffed Socks

Socks are just for feet, right? Wrong! Here are some game ideas that use socks rolled up into balls or stuffed with beans. Try them out for great action game fun.

What You'll Need:

- ➤ dried beans—
  1/2 cup per stuffed sock
- ➤ plastic bags or baggies—1 per stuffed sock
- ➤ twist-ties—1 per stuffed sock
- ➤ rubber bands—1 per stuffed sock
- ➤ medium or large cardboard box
- ➤ scissors

- ➤ tape
- ➤ markers, crayons, or other art materials
- ➤ timer
- ➤ shoes or boots—
  5 or more; different sizes

Here's How to Make Them:

1. To make one Stuffed Sock, put one half cup of dried beans into a plastic bag or baggie. Squeeze out most, but not all of the air in the bag and seal the bag shut with a twist-tie.

2. Stuff the bag with the beans into the toe area of a clean sock.

3. Roll the rest of the sock around the stuffed toe area. Put a sturdy rubber band around each sock roll.

4. Repeat Steps 1–3 to make more Stuffed Socks.

5. To make a Stuffed Sock Toss Game, you will need a medium cardboard box. Tape the box shut. Have a grown-up helper cut four circles of different sizes in the top of the box. The smallest hole should be just a bit larger than the size of a Stuffed Sock.

6. Decorate the box with markers, crayons, construction paper, and other art materials. Draw a number from 1–4 by each hole, making the biggest hole worth one point and the smallest hole worth four points.

7. To play the game, stand several feet away from the box. Toss a Stuffed Sock and try to get it into one of the holes in the box. You and other players can keep track of points scored. You might want to set an timer and keep tossing until your time is up.

8. To play a Shoe Toss Game, dig out six or more shoes from your family's closets, including your shoes and grown-up shoes. Spread them out on the floor, stand several feet away from them, and try to toss a Stuffed Sock into one of the shoes. Bigger shoes are worth less points than larger shoes!

More Family Fun:

● Stuffed Socks are soft and safe for a fun game of catch with a partner!

● Try playing Stuffed Sock Tag. The game is played like regular tag, only everyone has to balance a Stuffed Sock on their head!

● Stuffed Sock Races are lots of fun—try running with a Stuffed Sock balanced on your head, held tightly between your knees, or balanced on a spoon!

● What makes a Stuffed Sock stuffed? Beans! Buy some bean seeds with your family and plant them indoors in paper cups filled with potting soil. Poke a hole in the bottom of the cups and put them on saucers or plastic lids for drainage. Give them plenty of water and sunlight. Watch your beans grow—when they get about four inches tall, plant them outdoors in a garden!

Toss-It!

Here's a game that will test how well you can play ringtoss! It takes a lot of patience, skill, and practice to be the King or Queen of Toss-It!

What You'll Need:

- ➤ cardboard box lid
- ➤ sharp knife or scissors—for a grown-up helper
- ➤ wooden clothespins—10
- ➤ crayons or markers
- ➤ rubber jar rings—5

147

Here's How to Make It:

1. Have a grown-up helper cut ten small holes in a strong cardboard box lid (you can also use a shoebox lid, but it's not as sturdy). The holes should line up in two rows of five holes each.

2. Place a wooden clothespin into each of the holes so that they stick up out of the holes.

3. With crayons or markers, write the numbers 1–10 on the lid next to each clothespin.

4. To play a Toss-It Game, put the Toss-It box on the floor. Stand several feet away from it.

5. You and another player can take turns tossing rubber jar rings at the box. Try to toss the rings over the clothespins and score the number of points shown by each pin. It's harder than it looks, though—the rubbery rings are very bouncy!

More Family Fun:

- Toss-It boxes are perfect for bedtime playing fun. Just put the box at the end of your bed and toss the rings!

- Try playing Toss-It blindfolded! Have a partner loosely tie a handkerchief or cloth around your head so you can't see, then point you toward the Toss-It box. Try your luck!

- An exciting variation of Toss-It can be played in the dark, without a blindfold! Some hobby and craft supply stores carry bright fluorescent glow-in-the-dark paints. Paint the clothespins and numbers on your Toss-It box with the special paints. Dab glow-in-the-dark dots on the rubber jar rings, too. Shine a bright light on the paint so it absorbs a lot of light, then shut off the lights and play a glowing game of Toss-It—it's awesome fun!

- For a new slant on the game, have a grownup help you hang the Toss-It box on a wall or on a doorknob! Now you have to toss the rings so they hang on the clothespin pegs.

- Ringtoss games are found in most carnivals and fairs. Go on a Family Carnival Outing and take a trip to a carnival or county fair—ride the rides, play ringtoss and other fun games, and eat something sweet and sticky!

Sticky Stuff

Velcro is a great material that helps two things "stick" to each other. Now you can use amazing, "sticky" Velcro to make two games that will test your throwing and catching skills!

What You'll Need:

- ping-pong balls—2 or more
- self-adhesive Velcro dots— available at most fabric stores
- cardboard—2 feet square
- flannel, wool, or felt—2 feet square piece or bigger
- scissors
- tape or glue
- markers or fabric paint

150

Here's How to Make It:

1. To make a Sticky Stuff Dartboard, you need a two-foot square piece of cardboard. You can also lay a dinner plate on the cardboard and use a pencil to trace around it if you'd like your dartboard to be a circle instead of a rectangle.

2. Tape or glue a piece of flannel, wool, or felt material to the cardboard. You might want to make different scoring areas on your dartboard by taping or gluing different colors of felt to the cardboard. Make the different target areas circles or different shapes.

3. Use markers or fabric paints to draw different scoring areas (if you haven't used different colors of fabric). Use marker or fabric paints to put a number in each scoring area—if your "dart" lands in that area, you score those points!

4. Now get your "darts" ready by sticking self-adhesive Velcro dots at different spots around ping-pong balls.

5. Set up your Sticky Stuff Dartboard on the floor or lean it against a sofa or wall. A grownup can even help you attach a gummed picture-hanging eyelet so you can hang it on a wall or door!

6. You and a partner can take turns throwing your ping-pong ball "darts" at the dartboard. If you throw the darts just right, the Velcro dots will stick to the fabric on the board! You only score points when your dart sticks to a scoring area.

151

7. To make a Sticky Stuff Catcher's Mitt, tape or glue a piece of flannel, wool, or felt material to an eight-inch circle of cardboard.

8. Tape or glue the two edges of a one-inch strip of cardboard to the back of the mitt. Make sure the strip is long enough so you can comfortably slip your hand under it!

9. Make more mitts to play catch with friends. Or take turns and have a partner throw a Velcro-dotted ping-pong ball your way. Try to make it stick to your mitt!

More Family Fun:

- Make up different rules for your Sticky Stuff Dartboard. Label one section of the dartboard "Lose 1 Turn" and another section "Oops!" If you hit an "Oops!" area, you lose all your points—or whatever rule you'd like to make up!
- Paint your dartboard target areas with bright fluorescent glow-in-the-dark paints (available at some hobby and craft supply stores). Dab glow-in-the-dark dots on the ping-pong balls, too. Shine a bright light on the paint so it absorbs a lot of light, then shut off the lights and play a glowingly awesome game of Sticky Stuff Darts!

● Play a silly version of Sticky Stuff by looping the catcher's mitt through your belt. To catch the ball, you'll have to move your entire body in front of the ball! For the ultimate challenge, attach the mitt behind you so you have to catch backwards!

● Go to the library and check out books on baseball, softball, lacrosse, and other sports. Go on a Family Sports Night Outing to watch a high school or college team play baseball. The players don't use Velcro, but they can sure catch balls!

Fun-Time Bowling

Need to put a smile on a gloomy day? Try this new spin on the old game of bowling—it's an indoors game you can make and play!

What You'll Need:

- ➤ empty milk cartons—10 or more
- ➤ a ball—any kind will do
- ➤ tape, paste, or glue
- ➤ construction paper
- ➤ crayons or markers
- ➤ glitter, fabric scraps, feathers, or other art materials
- ➤ scissors

Here's How to Make It:

1. Get ten or more empty milk cartons—make sure they're rinsed out and dry inside before you begin.

2. Cut out construction paper and tape it around each carton. Color on the construction paper with markers or crayons. Use craft materials to make the milk cartons awesome, silly, weird, or great! Use your imagination with yarn, fabric and felt pieces, ribbon, glitter, feathers, pom-poms, and more.

3. When you've finished decorating the milk cartons, set them up in a line or in a group on the floor. Now you're ready for bowling! Stand or sit away from the milk cartons. Take a ball and roll it—see how many milk cartons you can knock down. Pick up the cartons you tipped over and set them aside. Keep rolling the ball and clearing away the cartons until you've gotten them all.

4. If you're playing with friends or other members of the family, see how many milk cartons each of you can knock down with one roll of the ball. Another way to play Fun-Time Bowling is to draw a different number on each milk carton. Add up the points on the milk cartons you knock down. The highest score wins.

More Family Fun:

- After all the fun of making and playing your bowling game, you just might be ready to try a family or neighborhood outing to a real bowling alley! Bowling is also a great outing for a birthday party.

But back to your home game...

- Instead of milk cartons, try decorating juice boxes and paper towel or toilet paper tubes—mix them up for different heights and shapes!
- Knock Down the Castle—Decorate milk cartons like parts of a castle (towers, walls, drawbridge). Stack them up to make a castle, then bowl it over!
- Stop the Monsters—Decorate paper towel and toilet paper tubes with big arms, gangs, googly eyes, and feet.
- Funny Bowling Bugs—Little juice boxes can make cute creepy-crawlies. Stick pipe cleaners into the hole at the top to make antennae, add feathers, and stick several pipe cleaner arms out from the sides.
- Cartoon Bowling Buddies—Decorate milk cartons to look like the Sesame Street gang, the Muppet Babies, Disney characters, or other favorite cartoon pals.

Let the Games Begin!

With very few supplies, you can help organize a Family or Neighborhood Olympics. There are a zillion and one ideas for games and activities that you can combine into one fun-filled event!

What You'll Need:

- balloons—lots of them, all shapes and sizes
- timer
- string—10 feet long
- chairs—2
- garden hose and water
- swimwear
- towels

- spoon
- paper plates
- scissors
- dowel rods
- crayons or markers
- index cards
- tape or glue
- old magazines

Here's How to Do It:

1. The Balloon Bounce—Each player has a balloon, or players can take turns with one balloon. The rules can be made so that either one hand or both hands can be used. Players must keep bouncing a balloon in the air while someone counts the number of bounces—set a timer to one minute to limit the bouncing action! Counting stops at the end of one minute or when the balloon hits the ground.

2. The Ring Fling—With scissors, carefully cut out the middle sections of strong paper plates so all that remains is the outer circular edge of the plates—these are the rings! Players can decorate their rings with crayons or markers so everyone knows who they belong to. Now set up your ring tossing area. If you are playing indoors, set up tall household objects on the floor, such as candles in candlesticks, tall bottles, or glasses. If you are playing outdoors, put dowel rods or other stakes into the ground. Set up a throwing line. Each player must stay behind the line and toss a ring around the dowel or object or land as close to one as possible. If you want, you can change the rules to allow more than one toss per turn.

3. Balloon Volleyball—Tie a ten-foot piece of string to the top of two chairs and separate the chair so that the string is pulled tight. Balloon Volleyball should be played outdoors, but you can play indoors if an grownup moves the furniture out of the way. The game can be played by teams or by two players. Hit a balloon back and forth until it hits the ground. Each side can keep hitting the balloon into the air any number of times—just so one of the hits gets the balloon over the string! Points are scored as in regular volleyball. You can also add ping-pong paddles or badminton rackets as extra equipment for hitting the balloon.

4. The Animal Race—Using scissors, cut out pictures of different animals from old magazines. Tape or glue them to index cards—one animal per card. Make about ten animal cards, or more if you'd like. Players line up at the starting line and race to the finish line, balancing a blown-up balloon or a potato between their knees while they carefully creep towards the end. If you drop the balloon or potato, you have to start over. But where do the animal cards come in? Before you begin, you must draw an animal card from the pack. Then you have to imitate the animal, complete with sound effects, while racing. Imagine balancing a balloon between your knees, flapping your arms like wings and yelling, "Tweet-tweet!"

5. The Balloony Spoony Race—It's as silly as its name, too! Players line up at the starting line and race to the finish line, but they need to balance a blown-up balloon on a spoon while they carefully creep towards the end. Racers start over if their balloon drops, and they can't hold onto their balloons or use their hands to recapture stray balloons—they can only use their spoons. Players can all race against each other, players can race one at a time and be timed by a watch or stopwatch, or players can form teams and turn the race into a relay event, passing off the spoon and balloon from one team member to another. Ping-pong balls, potatoes, and other small balls can be substituted for balloons. Paper plates can also be substituted for spoons (balloons must stay on the plates while racing). Add obstacles to make the race harder—for example, you could make it so players have to crawl through a large cardboard box.

6. The Hose Jump—Definitely for outdoor Olympic fun! Players wear swimwear. Turn on a garden hose and have a grown-up helper spray a stream of water about one foot off the ground. Players take turns jumping over the water—they must clear it. Anyone who hits the stream of water during their jump is retired—the agony of defeat! When all have jumped the first height, raise the hose another six inches or so. Keep raising the height of the hose until only one player is left! You can also reverse the game and call it Hose Limbo. Players start by going under the stream of water (it starts out high and ends up quite close to the ground). Players must not touch the stream, and they can walk, wiggle, crawl or flatten themselves any way they want. Be sure players bring towels to dry off afterwards!

More Family Fun:

Olympic "sports" make fun events for any family gathering, neighborhood party, or birthday celebration! Here are some more Olympic ideas:

● Make award ribbons, like Olympic medals, from construction paper. Cut out circles of white construction paper and color them with gold, silver, and bronze crayons. Punch a hole in the top of each "medal" and loop ribbon through it—just like in the real Olympics! Make other awards in different colors for fun categories like "Silliest Racer," "Most Wet," or "Most Popped Balloons." Make sure everyone gets some kind of medal!

● There are many activities and games in this book that can also be used in your Family or Neighborhood Olympics.

● Add other balancing games to your Olympics events! Have races where players have to carefully balance paper plates or feathers on their heads. Make it more difficult by balancing something on your head while holding something in each hand—try a paper plate on your head while you're holding a water balloon in each hand!

● Go to the library and check out books on the Olympics and your favorite sports and sports stars!

Goofy Golf

You can have great fun with your family and friends by setting up your own Goofy Golf course. You can even make your own golf clubs and tricky traps!

What You'll Need:

- ➤ giftwrap paper tubes, yardsticks, or broomsticks— 1 for each player
- ➤ stiff sponges—1 for each player
- ➤ rubber bands—1 for each player
- ➤ whiffle ball, ping-pong ball, or other small ball— 1 for each player
- ➤ medium or large cardboard box
- ➤ construction paper
- ➤ scissors
- ➤ tape

- ➤ markers or crayons
- ➤ empty yogurt containers or other plastic containers and lids— 3 or more
- ➤ old wire coat hangers— 3 or more
- ➤ aluminum foil pie pans— 3 or more
- ➤ household objects—like toys, flowerpots, big balls
- ➤ watch or stopwatch

Here's How to Make It:

1. Wrap a sturdy rubber band twice around a stiff sponge.

2. Slide a giftwrap paper tube, yardsticks, or broomsticks through the rubber band to attach it to the sponge. Now you have a Goofy Golf Club! Make one club for each player, or plan to share the club when each player takes a turn.

3. You can set up your Goofy Golf Course inside the house or outdoors—it's up to you! For an inside course, be sure to use a ping-pong ball, Nerf ball, or other soft ball to hit with your golf club. Don't hit the ball too hard so that it damages furniture or hits breakable objects!

4. To set up an inside course, turn three or more empty yogurt containers or other plastic containers on their sides for holes. Cut out construction paper flags and tape them to each container. Use markers or crayons to number each flag in your course so you can aim for the holes in order. Use furniture and other household objects as obstacles to shoot around or under! Ask a grownup if you can go from room to room.

5. To make one of the holes for your course, cut a hole in each side of a medium or large cardboard box. Decorate the box with construction paper, markers, and crayons. Draw a growling animal or giant with a big open mouth around each hole. Now try to shoot the ball into a dinosaur's mouth!

6. You can also play Goofy Golf outside. Set up plastic container lids on the ground and use these as tees. Put your balls in them and start from these spots. A few feet away from each tee, have a grownup use old wire coat hangers to make wire hoops to stick into the ground, like in croquet. Cut out construction paper flags and tape them to the hoops. Use markers or crayons to number each flag in your course. Hit your ball through the hoop and make a hole-in-one!

7. You can also use three or more empty yogurt containers or other plastic containers for holes. Set them on their sides in the grass, on the sidewalk, or on the patio. Ask a grownup to dig small holes in the grass and place the containers in the holes, tops level with the ground—now you've got real golf holes! Stick coat hanger hoops or stakes into the ground near each hole. Tape construction paper flags to the wires so you'll see where the holes are. You can also dig shallow holes and set aluminum foil pie pans into the ground near your golf holes. Fill them with water or sand and you have a tricky trap for your ball! Use toys and other household objects as obstacles to shoot around or under.

8. The cardboard box you made in Step 5 above also makes a good outdoor golf hole!

9. Gather your family and friends for a game of Goofy Golf. Keep track of how many hits it took you to put your ball through the hoop or into the hole. Count up scores and the player with the fewest hits wins!

More Family Fun:

● Here's a game called Fast Golf! Instead of counting the number of strokes it takes you to reach each hole, use a watch or stopwatch and see how fast you can get through the entire Goofy Golf Course. If you're playing alone, keep trying to beat your fastest time. If you're playing with others, the player with the fastest time through the course is the winner.

● Go with your family on a Family Mini-Golf Outing! Play a game of miniature golf at a real mini-golf course. The obstacles at these courses are very tricky, so keep the game fun by limiting the highest score on any hole to ten strokes.

● Visit a real golf course! It's fun to be with a grownup who plays golf. You'll get a lot of good walking exercise as you follow the ball around the course. Can you see where it lands after each hit? Maybe you can even help steer a golf cart—it's like a small car!

● Learn more about the game of golf at the library! Check out books with your family on golf, golf courses, the history of the game, and stories about great men and women golfers.

Rock 'n' Rollers

Dice are those 6-sided cubes that players roll to play many games. Here's a way to make Big Dice so you can really rock 'n' roll the next time you play!

What You'll Need:

- ➤ milk cartons—4; use the half-gallon size
- ➤ white or brown wrapping paper
- ➤ clear contact paper
- ➤ pencil

- ➤ ruler
- ➤ tape
- ➤ crayons or markers
- ➤ scissors

Here's How to Make Them:

1. Get four empty milk cartons—make sure they're rinsed out and dry inside before you begin. Have a grown-up helper open the tops of the milk cartons.

2. Measure a spot three inches from the bottom of each carton and draw a pencil line around the carton with a ruler. With scissors, cut along the lines. Throw away the top portion of each milk carton. The bottom part is what you'll use for your Big Dice!

3. Next, you're going to use two milk carton bottoms to make one Big Die. Take one milk carton bottom. Starting at the open end, cut a two-inch slit along each of the four corners. Gently press the sides of the slit carton together so that it can easily slide into an unslit milk carton bottom. Now you have a cube, with six complete sides and no open ends!

4. Repeat Step 3 for the remaining two milk carton bottoms. Now you have two Big Dice!

5. Your grown-up helper can help you wrap each Big Die with plain white or brown wrapping paper. Wrap it just like a present! Tape the paper snugly to each die.

6. Use crayons or markers to mark the six sides of each die with anything you'd like: the numbers 1–6, pictures, animals, words, colors, shapes, instructions (like "Lose One Turn" or "Go Back Three Spaces"). Mark both dice with the same markings!

7. To protect the six faces of your Big Dice, cover each face with clear contact paper. Trim off any excess with scissors.

8. Now you're ready to roll! Use your Big Dice instead of the small dice included with many board games—they're a lot more fun to play with.

More Family Fun:

● Play a Big Dice Match Game! Players roll the dice to make matches. The most matches within a certain amount of time or within a certain number of rolls wins.
● Play a Big Dice Math Game! See if you can add or multiply the numbers on the dice together.

● Mark different alphabet letters on your dice (so that they don't match), and play Big Dice Word Games! Think of words that start with the letters you throw. You can even make the letters initials for silly pretend names, like "Ant Princess" for A/P; "Bonnie Dishwasher" for B/D; and "Petunia Smartypants" for P/S. See how silly you can get!

● Get creative and make up your own board game. Draw out playing squares and decorate a piece of posterboard. Write different messages on some of the squares, like "Big Trap! Lose One Turn" or "Go Back to Start." You can use Big Dice with numbers on them, numbers and directions, or even colors (if you put the same colors on your playing squares). Name your new game and introduce it to your family!

● Make a stretch-and-twist game! First, make Big Dice with colors on each face. Then, for each of the six colors, take four sheets of paper, and on each sheet, draw a big dot in the matching color. You will need twenty-four sheets in all. Cover them with clear contact paper. Put the sheets down on a kitchen or hardwood floor. Tape each sheet to the floor with masking tape within a six-foot square playing area, and be sure to mix up all the colors. Take off your shoes and you're ready to play! Choose one person to be the Big Dice Roller. After rolling, players must touch a sheet with the same two colors that have come up on the dice. For example, if you roll a yellow and a green, you have to touch both a yellow and a green sheet with parts of your body—you might have to have a foot touching a yellow sheet and a hand touching a green sheet. Keep playing until all the players get tangled up in the playing area, or until there's only one who hasn't fallen over!

Off to the Races!

Here is a quiet way to race around in a fast sports car, go riding on the back of a huge polar bear, or go sailing to far-off places in a hot air balloon!

What You'll Need:

- construction paper—13 sheets
- old magazines
- cardboard
- tape or glue

- scissors
- crayons or markers
- 1 die or 1 Big Die
  (see page 167)

Here's How to Make It:

1. From old magazines, cut out pictures of different objects that move, like a horse, car, airplane, hot air balloon, or elephant. Tape or glue these on cardboard and cut them out. These are your Off to the Races playing pieces! Make one for each of your players.

2. Have some friends help you cut out one hundred rectangles from thirteen sheets of construction paper—that's a lot of cutting! The rectangles should each be about two inches by three inches. Helpful Hint: A quick way to get a lot of squares that size is to fold a sheet of paper in half, then in half again, then in half again. With scissors, cut a little bit off all four edges of the folded paper, and you'll get eight fast rectangles!

3. With crayons or markers, number each construction paper rectangle. Number them 1 through 100.

4. Now set up your racetrack! Lay the paper rectangles on the floor and place them in number order, from 1 to 100. You can space the rectangles out so they travel all around the room and form a circle. You can even have them go from one room to another—even up stairs (but be careful playing on stairs!).

5. Gather your friends and family together and have them all play Off to the Races. Every player picks one of the playing pieces you made in Step 1. Put all the pieces on space # 1. Roll a die or a Big Die to see who gets to take the first turn—the highest number goes first.

6. Each player takes turns rolling the die. Move the piece the number of miles indicated on the die.

7. If you land on someone else's space, you get to send that player back to the beginning again—oh, no!

8. The first player to reach the last space—100—by an exact roll of the die is the winner of the race.

More Family Fun:

● This is a fun game because there's always the threat of being sent back to the beginning—and races are always exciting! You can change or add rules to the game. Maybe you don't think someone should have to start all over again when you land on their square—maybe you can just send them back ten spaces.

● You can play this game with partners, too. If you land on your partner's space, you block all other players from passing you! Only one player in a team has to reach 100 for the team to win.

● It's fun to lay out the paper spaces of this game so that they go all over the house! Go under chairs, up sofas, around corners, and through tunnels that you can make with pillows.

● Go to the library with your family and check out books about racing. Look for your favorite racing animals, racing vehicles, and racing superstars. You can even rent a movie about racing for the whole family to enjoy (there are some good ones that feature wacky vehicles and silly, impossible races over long distances)!

Jug Hands

Do you ever wish you had giant hands so you could catch every ball that comes your way? Here's a project that will give you those big hands for great catching!

What You'll Need:

➤ plastic milk jugs—2 or more; use the gallon size with a handle on the side

➤ small balls or Stuffed Socks (see page 144)

➤ sharp knife or scissors— for a grown-up helper

175

Here's How to Make Them:

1. Get an empty milk jug—make sure it's rinsed out and dry inside before you begin.

2. Have a grown-up helper cut the milk jug in half, horizontally. The bottom of the milk jug can be used to store toys, blocks, and other items. But the top—the part with the handle—is what you'll use for Jug Hands!

3. Your helper should make sure that there are no sharp or rough edges left on the cut milk jug.

4. Repeat Steps 1–3 to make other Jug Hands jugs.

5. To play a Jug Hands Game, you and a partner will each have a Jug Hands jug. Hold it by the handle so that the open end is facing up.

6. Now try tossing a ball back and forth with your partner. Using only your Jug Hands jug to catch and throw the ball, see how many catches you and your partner can make before someone drops the ball. Keep trying to break your best record!

7. Try playing a game of Jug Hands catch using different objects: ping-pong balls, Stuffed Socks, tennis balls, or small rubber balls.

More Family Fun:

- Bring your Jug Hands jug to the beach—it makes a great sand scooper!
- Try a Jug Hands Wet Race! Have your grown-up helper poke a large hole in the cap of your milk jug with a hammer and nail. Snap or screw on the top, hold Jug Hands with the cap facing down, and fill Jug Hands with water from the garden hose. You and a friend can have a wet and wild water race or relay with Jug Hands dripping all over the place!
- Play Jug Hands Basketball! Have a partner stand still, holding Jug Hands upright. Try to toss a Stuffed Sock into the Jug Hands for two points! Take turns holding and shooting baskets.
- Jug Hands is made from a milk jug, but have you ever wondered how milk got to the store in the first place? Go to the library and check out books on milk, dairy products, and grocery stores! Go on a Family Farm Outing and visit a dairy farm—be sure to pet the cows!

Swing Ball

A pendulum is a weight that swings back and forth on a long cord or rod. You can make your own pendulum and play some great games!

What You'll Need:

- ➤ Stuffed Sock beanbag (see page 144)
- ➤ string, yarn, or elastic
- ➤ nail or thumbtack
- ➤ hammer
- ➤ blocks
- ➤ Fun-Time Bowling cartons (see page 154)
- ➤ balloons

Here's How to Make It:

1. Make one Stuffed Sock beanbag.

2. You will be playing Swing Ball in a doorway. Have a grownup help you hammer a small nail or thumbtack to the top of the door frame in the center of the doorway!

3. Tightly tie one end of a piece of string, yarn, or elastic around the Stuffed Sock.

4. Have your helper hold up the string, yarn, or elastic so that it reaches from the nail or thumbtack in the center of the door frame. Ask your helper to cut the string, yarn, or elastic so that the Stuffed Sock will hang about two to three inches off the floor.

5. Your helper can now tightly tie the string, yarn, or elastic around the nail or thumbtack. You're ready to play Swing Ball!

6. You and a partner sit on opposite sides of the doorway, facing each other. Play catch by swinging the ball back and forth. Try a variation where you can't hold on to the Swing Ball—pretend it's a Hot Potato and bat it away fast!

179

More Family Fun:

- Place blocks on the floor near your Swing Ball area. Build them into towers and other buildings. When you want to build something new, use Swing Ball to crash into the buildings and knock them down!

- Play Swing Ball Bowling by setting up Fun-Time Bowling cartons in the doorway area by your Swing Ball! (See page 154) See how many pins you can knock down with one swing.

- Substitute a balloon for a Stuffed Sock on the end of your Swing Ball cord! This will make the game entirely different (and better for younger children, too).

- Hang your Swing Ball from a tree branch and play an outdoors version of this game of catch. It's a great game for outside because you don't have to chase stray balls or worry about them rolling into the street!

- For some wet fun, play Swing Ball from a tree branch outdoors, but instead of using a Stuffed Sock, tie a water balloon on the end of the string, yarn, or elastic. Now play a game of catch—but be careful!

Spider Webs

Are spiders too creepy and crawly for you? Well, in this game, you must pretend to be a spider. Untangle your colorful spider web and find a special surprise!

What You'll Need:

- ➤ balls of yarn—various colors
- ➤ scissors
- ➤ construction paper
- ➤ crayon or markers

- ➤ tape
- ➤ wrapped candies or treats—
  1 for each player

Here's How to Make Them:

1. Spider Webs should be played indoors in one or two rooms.

2. Count how many players you will have playing the game. You will need one spider web for each player.

3. You and a grown-up helper can make the webs by cutting a piece of yarn about twenty or thirty feet long for each player. The game is easier to play if you have different colors, but if you only have one color of yarn, that's fine. (If you don't have any yarn, string works fine, too!)

181

4. Cut out small squares, rectangles, or other shapes from
construction paper and tape one to the end of each piece of yarn.
Use crayons or markers to write the first name of a player on each
cut-out shape.

5. Tie a small wrapped candy or other treat to the other end of
the piece of yarn.

6. Before you play the game, spin your Spider Web! You and
your helper will weave each piece of yarn loosely around the one or
two rooms you're using for the game. Wrap them around chairs,
table legs, and under sofas. Crisscross yarn around other pieces of
yarn. Make a big jumbled web with all the pieces of yarn!

7. To play the game, send all players around the game room or rooms to find their name tags. When everyone has found the right tag, the game begins.

8. Each player has to untangle his or her piece of yarn and find the treat at the end of it. The first player to reach his or her treat is the Spider Webs winner!

More Family Fun:

- Spider Webs makes a great Halloween game! Spiders and this spooky holiday naturally go together. Make webs with black and orange pieces of yarn. Instead of wrapped treats, attach rubber spiders or other creepie crawlies to the end of the yarn webs.
- Play Spider Webs at a birthday or other family party! Instead of wrapped treats, attach goodie bags for each guest to the end of the yarn webs.
- Go with your family to the library and check out books on different kinds of spiders. Find out all about what they eat, which ones make good pets, which ones are very dangerous, and how spiders spin their amazing webs!

Family Fun

Quiet(er) Games

Activity Book

I Want My Mummy!

Here's a game where you get to turn a family member or a friend into a real live mummy. Put on some "wrap" music and have a lot of fun!

What You'll Need:

➤ toilet paper rolls—1 roll for
every 2 players; different colors;
unscented is best

➤ tape

Here's How to Do It:

1. I Want My Mummy! is best played with six or more players. Divide all the players into pairs.

2. Pick one player in each pair to be the Mummy. The other will be the Mummy Maker.

3. Give each Mummy Maker a roll of toilet paper and some tape.

4. Tell the Mummy Makers, "We have found some Egyptian mummy wrapping cloth. It is very old and very delicate." Tell them that they will be in a race with the other Mummy Makers to completely wrap their Mummies from head to foot—but no wrapping around the face. Completely wrap the legs, the feet, the arms, the hands, and the rest of your Mummy's body. If the mummy wrap breaks, you must repair it with tape. The object is to wrap your Mummy with one continuous sheet of mummy wrap paper!

5. A grown-up helper or another player can play some music on the radio, record player, cassette player, or CD player. Maybe you can play some mummy "wrap" music—oooh, that was a bad joke! Or, since mummies are often turned into monsters in scary movies, it might be fun to play spooky music.

187

6. When everyone is ready, you can yell, "I Want My Mummy!" All the Mummy Makers start to wrap their Mummies with toilet paper.

7. The first team with a completely wrapped Mummy wins!

8. If you have enough toilet paper left, or extra rolls of paper on hand, teams can trade off—the Mummy Maker now becomes the Mummy and the Mummy becomes the Mummy Maker. Play I Want My Mummy! again.

More Family Fun:

● This is a great game that's fun to play at a family or neighborhood Halloween party! Make construction paper ribbons and award prizes to teams for "Creepiest Mummy," "Silliest Mummy," "Messiest Mummy," "Neatest Mummy," and so on.

● Instead of toilet paper, play I Want My Mummy! with different colors of crepe paper streamers! Crepe paper is sturdier for wrapping and may be better for younger players.

● Go with your family to the library and check out books on ancient Egypt, mummies, the pyramids, the pharoahs (Egyptian rulers), the Nile River, and the Egyptian gods and goddesses. Learn all about how and why mummies were made!

● Do you live close to a museum with mummies? If you do, have your family take you on a trip to see the mummies! Usually they are displayed with other objects from ancient Egypt, like temple carvings, jewelry, household objects and other works of art. Bring along some drawing paper and crayons or colored pencils. Draw pictures of what you see, then you can take them home and show them to your friends!

Picture Peeking

This is a game that's fun to make and very mysterious to play! It's a great guessing game that you can play with your family and friends.

What You'll Need:

- ➤ paper—20 or more sheets, each the same size, plus 1 sheet that's larger than the rest
- ➤ old magazines
- ➤ tape or glue
- ➤ scissors

Here's How to Make It:

1. Cut out pictures of different objects, people, animals— anything you like—from old magazines. Some can be unusual, like dinosaurs, while others can be simple everyday things like a lamp or a stove.

2. Tape or glue one picture on a sheet of paper. Collect about twenty or more different sheets of paper, each with its own picture on it. The size of these picture sheets should all be the same. 8 1/2-by-11-inch sheets of paper are ideal, but you can even use smaller index cards for your pictures.

3. Now prepare a special "cover sheet." This sheet of paper should be almost twice the size of the picture sheets. You should be able to completely cover the sheet and move it around on top of the picture sheets. Near the middle of the cover sheet, cut a small 1/4-inch hole.

4. You're ready to play Picture Peeking! First, you are going to be the Picture Hider. The other player will be the Picture Peeker. Turn the picture sheets over, picture side down. Let the Picture Peeker choose one of the pictures, without looking at it.

5. You get to see the whole picture! Then, without showing it to the other player, hide the picture with the cover sheet. Move the cover sheet around so that a small piece of the picture shows through the cover sheet hole!

6. Let the Picture Peeker peek at the picture by looking at it through the hole. Can the player guess what it is? Allow three guesses. If the guesses are all wrong, move the cover sheet a little bit so that the hole is over another area of the picture. Again, allow three more guesses. If you stump the Picture Peeker, you get a point! If the Picture Peeker guesses correctly after peeking at the picture, they get a point.

7. Take turns being the Picture Peeker and the Picture Hider.

More Family Fun:

● This is a great game that everyone in your family will enjoy playing. Keep the cover sheet with just one hole for older players and grownups. You might want to make an easier cover sheet for younger Picture Peekers—cut three small holes near the middle part of the cover sheet for easier peeking!

● Go to the library and check out books on art and famous artists. There are some great color photographs of famous paintings in books, too. Use crayons and markers and try to draw your own masterpieces for the Picture Peekers game!

● Pictures are fun to look at. Go with your family to an art gallery and look at the works of art—without having to cover them up with paper!

● Have a grownup make two photocopies of each of your picture sheets, and you can play a Memory Matching Game! With 20 picture sheets, you have forty photocopies (two of each sheet). Play with only the photocopied sheets, not the originals. Shuffle all forty sheets and turn them upside down, hiding the pictures. Arrange the sheets in a big rectangle on the floor, five rows of eight sheets. Players take turns by turning over any two sheets of paper. If they match, keep them and continue to turn over two more sheets. Play continues until all the sheets are taken. The winner has the most sheets. See if you have a good memory—try to remember where the matches are!

Stone Game

Native Americans created games that involved rolling stones or pebbles that were carved or painted with different symbols. Now you can make your own game from stones, too!

What You'll Need:

- ➤ small stones or pebbles—21
- ➤ paper towels
- ➤ nail polish or paint
- ➤ paintbrush
- ➤ empty coffee can

- ➤ construction paper
- ➤ crayons or markers
- ➤ scissors
- ➤ tape

Here's How to Make It:

1. Wash the stones or pebbles under running water. Put them on paper towels and let them dry well.

2. Using either nail polish or paints and a paintbrush, paint an "X" on seven of the stones.

3. Paint a "Z" on seven of the stones.

4. Paint an "O" on seven of the stones.

5. Let the nail polish or paint dry well on each stone.

6. Cut a piece of construction paper as tall as an empty coffee can and long enough to more than fit around the can.

7. Use crayons or markers to draw a "Nature Picture" on the construction paper strip. For example, you can draw a river, tree, flower, bird, star, sun, mountain, or animal.

8. Wrap the construction paper strip around the coffee can. Overlap the ends of the strip and tape them together.

9. Put the stones into the coffee can (make sure the nail polish or paint has dried first!).

10. Now you're ready to play the Stone Game! Each player reaches into the can and pulls out one stone. When all the stones have been taken from the can, each player divides up his or her stones into "X," "Z," and "O" piles. The player with the most stones with one kind of letter on them is the winner. Keep playing for a certain period of time to see who is the overall Stone Game winner.

More Family Fun:

● To collect your stones, go on a Family Rock Hunt Outing! Travel to a hillside, mountain, seashore, beach, riverbank, or other natural area and hunt for stones for the Stone Game. Start a rock collection and display your best stones!

● If you'd like, add more stones to your can so the Stone Game lasts longer! (You must add stones only in multiples of three, so that the number of stones with each of the three letters stays the same.) Paint the stones with an "X," "Z" and "O," and let them dry well before playing with them.

● Use your Stone Game to play a traditional Japanese game called Jan-Ken-Pon or Jan-Kem-Po—Scissors, Paper, Stone! The "X" stones stand for Scissors, the "Z" stones stand for Paper, and the "O" stones stand for Stone. Two players take turns by drawing stones from the can:

— Scissors ("X") beats Paper ("Z") because scissors
   can cut paper;

— Paper ("Z") beats Stone ("O")
   because paper can wrap around stone; and

— Stone ("O") beats Scissors ("X")
   because a stone can dull scissors.

Each player gets a point when they "win" a round. No one gets a point if the same letters are drawn. Keep score and see who gets the most points!

● Play the Odd or Even Game with your stones! Sit with your fellow players in a circle. Everyone gets a sheet of paper and a pencil. Write "10" at the top of the paper—every player starts out the game with ten points. Next, pass the can filled with stones to the first player. That player reaches in the can and counts out an odd or even number of stones and puts them in a closed fist. "Odd or Even?" the first player asks the person sitting to his or her left in the circle. That player must then guess if there is an even or odd number of stones in the fist. If the guess is correct, that player keeps the same point total, but the player who picked the stones loses one point. If the guess was not correct, the player who picked the stones keeps the same point total, but the player who guessed wrong loses one point. Mark the point changes on your sheet of paper. The game continues around the circle until one player runs out of points. The player with the most points wins!

● Go with your family to the library and check out books on rocks, minerals, gemstones, volcanoes, mountains, and other stone subjects. See if you can name some of the stones in your Stone Game. Find out how they were made!

Presenting the Present

Here's a game that combines music, a group of four or more players, and a mysterious present that keeps getting passed around from one player to the next!

What You'll Need:

- ➤ small cardboard box or shoe box with lid
- ➤ gift wrap or white or brown wrapping paper
- ➤ crayons or markers
- ➤ tape

- ➤ scissors
- ➤ radio, record player, tape player, or CD player—and music!
- ➤ small prize, treat, or craft item
- ➤ old newspapers

Here's How to Make It:

1. Before playing the game, you get to pick a prize for the present! It can be a treat or a wrapped goodie. It can be a little present provided by a grownup (a good idea for birthday or other holiday parties). It can also be something you made from the arts & crafts projects in this book!

198

2. Put the prize in a small cardboard box or shoe box with lid. Wad up old newspapers and pack them around the prize so that it doesn't get broken or damaged when players Present the Present! Tape the box shut.

3. Have a grownup help you wrap the box with a layer of gift wrap or white or brown wrapping paper. Cut the paper to fit the box, fold it around the box, then tape it tight. If you're using plain white or brown paper, decorate the wrap with crayons or markers!

4. Now the fun part begins! Wrap several more layers of gift wrap or white or brown wrapping paper around the box. Wrap ten layers or more! Decorate each layer if you'd like. You can also alternate and keep one layer plain, decorate the next layer, keep the next one plain, and so on.

5. After you're done wrapping you can start the game. Players sit in a circle on the floor. Give the Present to one of the players.

6. Your grown-up helper is the Music Leader. The Music Leader starts the music (on a radio, record player, tape player, or CD

199

player—or maybe your helper can play the piano or other musical instrument!). The player with the present must quickly Present the Present to the next player in the circle.

7. The next player must quickly Present the Present to the next player. Each player quickly Presents the Present around the circle until the Music Leader stops the music!

8. The player who has the Present when the music stops gets to unwrap the first layer of gift wrap.

9. The Music Leader starts the music again and players continue to quickly Present the Present around the circle until the music stops. Another layer is unwrapped, and play continues.

10. When a player gets to unwrap the last layer of gift wrap, that person is the Present the Present winner—open the box and get your prize!

More Family Fun:

● For a sillier version of Present the Present, each player must quickly say "Here's the Present!" when they Present the Present to the next player. Everyone will get very giggly!

● After you play this game, set up chairs in a circle and play Musical Chairs. Put in one less chair than the number of players. The Music Leader plays music and everyone marches around the chairs. When the music stops, scramble to find a seat! The player without a seat gets to sit out and cheer on the others. Take out another chair and start the music and marching again. Keep eliminating players and taking out one more chair until it's down to two players and one chair. The winner is the one sitting in the chair when the music stops!

● Play Welcome the Water Balloon! For hot summer fun outdoors, all players can cool off in swimwear. Make up lots of water balloons and play the game the same way as Present the Present. Quickly pass a water balloon around the circle while the music plays, and stop passing when the music stops. You can play two ways: keep passing the balloon until it pops or drops...or the person caught with the water balloon has to sit on it and pop it!

● Help a grownup wrap and decorate presents for a family birthday or holiday party! Learn how to cut the wrap, fold it around a present, tie ribbons, and make bows.

● Make your own special giftwrap paper! Stamp pictures on plain brown or white wrapping paper sheets with potato stamps dipped in paint (see page 106). Let the sheets of stamped giftwrap dry completely, then wrap special presents for your family!

● Where did the custom of giving presents start? Go to the library with your family and do a little digging into presents, gifts, holidays, birthdays, and parties. See if you can unwrap the mystery of presents!

Puzzle Pick Up

Pick Up Sticks is a game children have played for many, many years. Here's a new twist to the game, combining the skill of picking up the sticks with the fun of putting puzzles together.

What You'll Need:

- ➤ old magazines
- ➤ white drawing paper
- ➤ posterboard
- ➤ white liquid glue
- ➤ ruler
- ➤ pencil
- ➤ scissors

Here's How to Make Them:

1. From an old magazine, cut out one entire page that catches your eye—it's best that the page be mostly pictures, like a photograph or product ad. Glue this page onto posterboard. Let it dry completely.

2. A grownup can help you with this next step. Use a ruler and pencil to draw a line dividing the picture in half horizontally (on an 8 1/2-inch-by-11-inch sheet, draw the line 5 1/2 inches up the page). Then lay the ruler at the top of the page and make a mark at each

1/4-inch interval. Lay the ruler at the bottom of the page and do the same thing. Now use the ruler to draw a pencil line connecting each mark at the top of the page with the one directly underneath it.

3. With scissors, cut out the 1/4-inch "sticks." On an 8 1/2-inch-by-11-inch picture, you are cutting out 68 sticks. This is how you turn your picture into a puzzle!

4. Now you can use these puzzle sticks to play Pick Up Sticks! Hold the puzzle sticks in one hand and rest the bottom of the sticks against the table of floor.

5. Let the sticks go, scattering over the table.

6. Try to pick up the puzzle sticks, one at a time. Be careful not to make another stick move when you're picking up a stick. If that happens, your turn is over!

7. Count how many sticks you pick up each turn. You can keep score, or just try to beat your personal record.

8. If you're playing with another person or a group, the player with the most pick-ups in one turn is the winner. Then everyone gets to try to put all the sticks together to form the puzzle picture!

More Family Fun:

- For a more challenging game and puzzle activity, cut out two sets of puzzle sticks and use both sets at the same time!
- Here's a new rule you can try: Players who successfully pick up puzzle sticks during their turn can keep them out of play, passing on the remaining sticks to the next person. Sticks taken out of play are then put on the table to begin building the puzzle picture. It's fun to pick up sticks, then fit them into a puzzle after your turn is over!
- You can play a more traditional game of Pick Up Sticks with popsicle or craft sticks, plastic straws, or toothpicks.
- Surprise a member of your family by drawing a special picture or message on a sheet of white drawing paper. Mount it on poster board and cut it out into a puzzle. Play the pick up game, then put the puzzle together. Imagine the wonderful gift when a message like "Happy Birthday, Mom—I Love You" is pieced together!

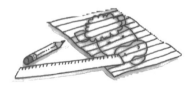

Big Bingo

Most grownups played Bingo when they were little, and many still play Bingo games. It's always been popular, but it's never quite been played this big before!

What You'll Need:

- milk cartons—
  4; use the half-gallon size
- white or brown wrapping paper
- clear contact paper
- pencil

- ruler
- tape
- posterboard
- crayons or markers
- scissors

205

Here's How to Make It:

1. The Big Dice instructions are on page 167. Make one Big Die for your Big Bingo game.

2. Use crayons or markers to mark the six sides of the die with the numbers 1–6, pictures of animals, words, colors, or shapes. Protect the six faces of your Big Die by covering each face with clear contact paper. Trim off any excess with scissors.

3. Draw a large rectangle, square, circle, triangle, or other shape on a piece of posterboard. Cut out your shape with scissors.

4. Place your shape on another piece of posterboard, trace around it with a pencil, then cut it out.

5. Using another shape, repeat Step 4 until you have a total of six different posterboard shapes.

6. Use crayons or markers to decorate your six pieces of posterboard to match the markings that you made on your Big Die. For example, if you drew a picture of a dog, a cat, a monkey, an elephant, a horse and a snake on the different faces of the Big Die, draw one of those animals on each sheet of posterboard. Now you have your Big Bingo Pieces!

7. Decorate the other side of your Big Bingo Pieces with crayons or markers. You can draw pictures or even write the word "BINGO!"

8. To play the game, gather all the players together and have each player spread out their Big Bingo Pieces on the floor beside them. Turn the pieces so the Big Die markings can be seen. Arrange the pieces in two rows of three pieces each!

9. One player is the Big Die Roller. He or she rolls the die and calls out what the roll was (or the roller can hold up the die for everyone to see). Each player turns over their matching Big Bingo Piece, so the decorated back side of the piece shows.

10. Play continues until one player has turned over all three cards in one of their rows. The winner should yell, "Big Bingo!"

More Family Fun:

● Set an timer and keep playing the game until the time is up. See which player has the most wins and give that person a construction paper crown—they're the Big Bingo King or Queen!

● Play Big Bingo without the Big Die. Cut out twenty-six construction paper squares and on each square mark the letters of the alphabet or the numbers 1–26. Put these Big Bingo Markers in a paper bag. Players make six Big Bingo Pieces, but they mark them with six letters or six numbers—whatever they pick! One player is the Big Bingo Caller, drawing markers from the bag. Players who have one of the letters or numbers called can turn over their pieces. The winner is the first to have all six pieces turned over!

● Go on a Family Car Trip and play Car Bingo! Players in the car each get a sheet of paper. Write the numbers 1–9 on each sheet. Players take turns spotting license plates from cars traveling on the same roadway. The player who spots the plate gets to pick one number from the plate and scratch it off their list. The first player who scratches off all nine numbers wins.

● Here's another version of Car Bingo. Before the car trip, each player makes a list of ten or more objects that are usually seen from a roadway, like a gas pump, restaurant, man with a beard, water tower, river, flag, garbage truck, or speed limit sign. Once the trip begins, players look for things on their list, call them out when they spot them, and scratch them off. Scratch off all the items on your list and you can yell, "Car Bingo!"

Shuffle Story Cards

Here are two game ideas to turn anyone into a storyteller. And there are no limits to the stories you can tell with these special Shuffle Story Cards!

What You'll Need:

- ➤ old magazines
- ➤ tape or glue
- ➤ index cards
- ➤ crayons or markers
- ➤ tape recorder and blank tape

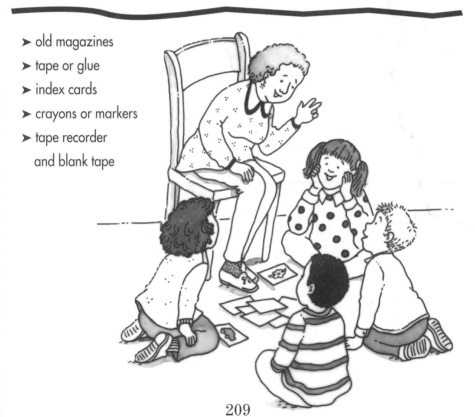

Here's How to Make
Shuffle Story Cards—Version 1:

1. Cut out lots of pictures from old magazines—interesting scenes, objects, people, or anything that catches your eye. The more pictures, the better.

2. Tape or glue each picture on its own index card.

3. Shuffle your Story Cards and mix them up well. Now you're ready to play the Shuffle Story Game!

4. Gather a group of "storytellers" together in a circle. Put the Shuffle Story Cards picture side down in the center of the circle.

5. You are the first storyteller. Pick a Shuffle Story Card from the deck. Look at it and take a little time to think about the picture. Then put it on the floor in front of you so that everyone in the circle can see it, too.

6. Make up the start of a story that ties in with the card. For example, the picture may be a picture of a boy eating a hotdog: "Once upon a time there was a boy named Sam. He was very hungry, so he ate a hotdog. It tasted good." Don't make your story too long—others in the circle will add to it!

7. The person to your left picks the next Shuffle Story Card, looks at it, and puts it down on the floor so everyone in the circle can see it. This person's job as storyteller is to continue to tell the story where you left off, but it has to tie in with the card he or she just drew! For example, the new picture shows an astronaut in a spacesuit: "After Sue finished her hotdog, she decided to blast off for a trip to the moon. When she got there, she started to explore!"

8. The next person picks the next Shuffle Story Card, and the story continues. Continue around the circle until it becomes your turn again. Pick a Shuffle Story Card, put it down in front of you, and it is your job as storyteller to finish the story, using the picture you just chose. The rule of this game is that whoever starts a story has to finish it!

Here's How to Make
Shuffle Story Cards—Version 2:

1. In this version, players in the circle do not tell stories. They make silly sentences! Cut out lots of pictures from magazines and this time, divide them into four different groups: People, Actions, Objects, and Places. Here are some examples of each:
— People might include pictures of a man in a suit, a little girl, a queen, a doctor, a truck driver, or a baby
— Actions might include pictures showing someone running,

211

playing basketball, sleeping, hitting a baseball, talking on
the telephone, cooking, or swimming

— Objects might include pictures of a soft drink, a cookie,
a car, a worm, a cat, a table, a tree, a lamp, a piano,
a bicycle, or a pickle

— Places might include pictures showing a park, an office,
a jail, a movie theater, a house, the moon, a closet, a
baseball stadium, or a school room

2. Tape or glue each picture on its own index card. Write on the
back of the card which of the four groups it belongs to—People,
Actions, Objects, or Places.

3. Instead of pictures, you can also take index cards and use
markers or crayons to write down your own People, Actions,
Objects, or Places—one on each card. Be sure to write on the back
of the card which group it belongs to.

4. Gather a group of "storytellers" together in a circle. Put the
Story Cards in four piles, according to grouping. Shuffle each pile
well, and put them picture-side or word-side down in the center of
the circle.

5. Take one card from the top of each deck, turn them over, and
put them in order: People, Actions, Objects, and Places. Then, read
your sentence to everyone. For example: A queen (Person)...hit a
baseball (Action)...with a pickle (Object)...on the moon (Place).
Another crazy combination might be: A baby...was cooking...a car
...in the park!

6. Everyone in the circle gets a chance to make silly sentences. With your Shuffle Story Cards, the sentence combinations are endless!

More Family Fun:

● To make your Shuffle Story time special, pass a tape recorder around the circle and have everyone record their turn. Play the tape back and hear the whole story!

● Go with your family on a Family Storytelling Outing! Visit the library or a children's bookstore during Story Hour or an author's reading.

● Check out your favorite stories from the library. Have a grown-up read them to you. If you are a good reader, maybe there's someone younger in your family or neighborhood that you can read to!

Maze Magic

With some index cards or construction paper and a few simple tools, you can make amazing mazes and crazy courses with your family and friends!

What You'll Need:

- ➤ index cards or construction paper
- ➤ pencil
- ➤ scissors
- ➤ crayons or markers
- ➤ ruler
- ➤ old newspapers

Here's How to Make It:

1. Use a ruler and pencil to measure out a one-inch square from an index card (they work best) or construction paper. Use scissors to cut it out. Use this square to trace more squares, or use your ruler to measure them out on index cards or construction paper.

2. Cut out sixty squares.

3. Divide the squares into ten different piles with six cards in each pile.

4. To make your Magic Maze Cards, use a ruler and a crayon or marker to draw the ten different marks shown in the picture. Draw each mark six times, on each of the six cards in your ten piles. Make sure that each line you draw reaches the ends of the squares! Draw over a sheet of old newspaper so you can draw off the square without drawing on a tabletop or floor. See how one mark is blank? Leave a pile of six squares completely blank.

5. Pick any two squares, except for a blank square, and draw a big dot or star on each. This will mark the Start and the End of your maze!

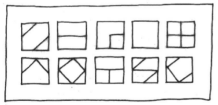

6. Take out the two marked squares, shuffle the rest of the cards, and mix them up well. Put them in one big pile in front of you. Lay down one of the marked cards as the Start of your maze. Pick up one card at a time from the deck and place it so the lines will connect with other squares you've already played. That's how you build your maze!

7. When you've put all the Maze Magic Cards together, place the last marked card to mark the End of the maze!

215

8. Use your finger to trace the maze from the Start to the End. Can you do it? See if someone else in your family can do it. Invite friends over to try out your maze and make their own. Try to amaze each other with real tricky ones!

More Family Fun:

● Keep adding more cards to your Magic Maze game! Make bigger and better mazes. Just keep adding cards in multiples of ten, so you can add one new card for each of the ten marks shown in the picture.

● Make Big Magic Maze Cards! Trace the ten marks onto large pieces of construction paper or on squares of posterboard. Lay them down to build big mazes. Use toy trucks and cars to travel on top of your maze—now they're roads!

● Mazes are fun because they're filled with tricky dead ends. Sometimes it's very easy to get lost before you get to the End. But getting lost in real life isn't fun at all. Have you ever been lost before? How did you feel? Here are some good ideas that can help you:

— Talk to the grownups in your family about getting lost. Know the safe places to play around your house and neighborhood. Make a plan to follow in case you get lost. Be sure to follow the safety rules you and your family discuss.

— Talk about special plans for staying together when you're on family trips or outings. Pick a place you can go to if you get separated from the rest of your family.

— If you get separated from your family in a big store, go to someone who works in the store and ask for help in finding your family.

— Learn your home address and phone number.

— Know how to spell the first and last names of the grownups in your family.

— Learn where the grownups in your family work.

— Learn to talk to grownups you can trust, like the police or family friends.

— Be polite to all grownups, but you have the right to say "No!" to anything a grownup says or does that makes you feel uncomfortable. Run away from grownups who are trying to get you to go with them—and yell for help, too!

— Tell a parent or another grownup you know and can trust that another grownup is bothering you or has done something to you that makes you feel uncomfortable.

— Know that a grownup who looks nice and acts friendly toward you may not be a person you can trust. Be careful at all times!

● There are many good books in the library on how to be safe when you're lost or how to be safe around grownups you don't know. Check out these books with your family, read them, and learn how to stay safe and happy!

Puzzle Fun

Puzzles are great entertainment for rainy days, quiet moments, and family times! Here are some puzzle ideas you can have fun making and putting together.

What You'll Need:

- ➤ map of the world or the United States
- ➤ clear contact paper
- ➤ pencil
- ➤ white liquid glue

- ➤ posterboard
- ➤ crayons or markers
- ➤ scissors
- ➤ manilla envelopes

218

Here's How to Make It:

1. Get a map of the world or the United States. You can use a color weather map from a newspaper, a map from an in-flight airline magazine, or a large map you purchase at a book or stationery store. If you use a map from the newspaper, cover it with clear contact paper to make it less messy to touch.

2. Glue the map to a large sheet of posterboard. When it dries, use scissors to trim the edges of the map even with the posterboard.

3. Now you're ready to turn the map into a puzzle. Learning all about the world or the United States is fun, but you might want to start simple and work up. For a world map, start by cutting out the different continents, or the large blocks of land. For the United States map, cut out four or five different blocks of states, or the fifty different blocks of land that form the United States. (If you live in Canada or another country, turn your maps into puzzles the same way!)

4. Mix up the puzzle pieces and see if you can put the map back together again. If you have any trouble, ask a grownup to help.

5. Soon you'll be learning all about maps. Try making your puzzle more difficult. Cut out different groups of countries from each continent on a world map. Cut out smaller groups of states on a United States map. Work up to cutting out different countries on the world map and separate states on the United States map (or the Canadian provinces or other state and regional groupings of your country)!

6. Store your map puzzles in a manila envelope for future play.

More Family Fun:

● Buy a map of your state, province, or territory. They're available at many service stations, drugstores, bookstores, and other retail outlets. Glue the map to posterboard, draw puzzle pieces with pencil (try drawing pieces along rivers and streams, highways, mountain ranges, and other map features), and cut along the lines. Put the map together and find where you live on the map!

● Draw a picture and turn it into a puzzle! Use markers, crayons, or paints and make a picture. Glue it to posterboard and cut the picture to size. Use a pencil to draw different puzzle shapes on your picture, or draw around people, objects and designs in your art. Cut them out and give them to a friend or family member to put together. Show off your great artwork!

● Collect funny jokes and riddles. Use markers and crayons to draw a picture that shows the funny part about a joke or the answer to a riddle. Have a grownup help you print out the funny part of the joke or the riddle's answer beside your picture. Glue the picture to posterboard and use a pencil to draw different puzzle shapes on your picture, or draw around people, objects and designs in your art. Tell a friend or family member your joke, or ask them your riddle. They will have to put your puzzle together to read the ending!

● Make Greeting Card Puzzles! Turn your greetings for holidays, birthdays, and special family times and occasions into art and words on a piece of paper. Turn it into a puzzle, slip the pieces into a nice envelope, and hand it to a special person—they'll love putting together your wonderful gift!

● Make Party Invitation Puzzles! Having a party or a big family or neighborhood event? Make a special invitation picture and write down all the party details on a piece of paper. A grownup can make photocopies of your picture, one copy for each guest. Glue the invitations to posterboard, color them with crayons or markers, and cut them up into puzzles. Slip the pieces into envelopes and hand-deliver these great invitations.

Checker Out

Here's a new game for two players that uses Big Dice and an old family favorite—checkers! The object is to be the first to move all your checkers off the board.

What You'll Need:

- ➤ milk cartons—
  4; use the half-gallon size
- ➤ white or brown wrapping paper
- ➤ clear contact paper
- ➤ tape
- ➤ crayons or markers
- ➤ checkerboard and checkers

Here's How to Make It:

1. The Big Dice instructions are on page 167. Follow the steps indicated to make two dice for your Checker Out game.

2. One die will be a Checker Move Die. Use crayons or markers to mark the six sides of the die with these checker moving directions:

      Move 1 Checker Ahead 1
      Move 1 Checker Ahead 2
      Move 2 Checkers Ahead 1
      Move 1 Checker Back 1
      Move 1 Checker Back 2
      Move 2 Checkers Back 1

3. The other die will be a Luck Die. Use crayons or markers to mark the six sides of the die with these good and bad luck directions:

> Send 1 Checker Back 1
> Send 1 Checker Back 2
> Checker Out 1 Checker!
> Piggyback Any 2 Checkers
> Move All Your Checkers Back 1
> Lose Next Turn

4. Protect the six faces of your Big Dice by covering each face with clear contact paper. Trim off any excess with scissors.

5. Set up the checkerboard for a game of Checker Out! Line up four black checkers on one end of the first row of squares. Line up four red checkers on the remaining squares in that row. Make two more rows of checkers the same way. All twelve black checkers should be together on one side; all twelve red checkers should be together on the other side.

6. Take turns rolling the Big Dice. Follow the directions indicated on both dice.

7. The directions that say "Move…" are telling you to move your checkers one or two squares ahead or back during your turn. You can move any checkers you want. When one of your checkers reaches the last row, take it off the board and yell, "Checker Out!" Checker Out all your checkers to win the game.

8. The directions that say "Send…" are telling you to move the other player's checkers during your turn. You can move any checkers you want. Try to pick checkers that are close to the last row so you can keep them from going Checker Out.

9. If you roll "Checker Out 1 Checker!" you can pick any of your checkers to take off the board. Great! Another good luck direction is "Piggyback Any 2 Checkers." When you roll that one, take one of your checkers off the board and put it on top of another one. Move both of those checkers together and, with luck, you will Checker Out both at once!

10. There are two bad luck directions you might roll: "Move All Your Checkers Back 1" and "Lose Next Turn." Sorry!

11. Keep rolling, moving checkers, and taking turns until one player is able to Checker Out all checkers.

More Family Fun:

● Instead of using a regular checkerboard and checkers, make a Big Checker Out Game! Tape pieces of red and black construction paper to make a Big Board. Cover empty half-gallon milk cartons or juice boxes with red and black construction paper to make Big Checkers (twelve red and twelve black).

● Use two different kinds of wrapped candy or treats as a yummy alternative to playing the game with checkers!

● Have a Checker Out Party with your family! Feature red and black food like radishes, red and black licorice, red hots, red peppers, catsup-covered burgers or meatloaf, salsa-covered tacos, tomato soup, open-faced peanut butter sandwiches covered with strawberry or red raspberry jelly, black olives, and fruit punch. Serve everything on a red checked tablecloth with red and black paper plates, cups, and napkins. After eating, play Checker Out and crown a Family Champion!

Family Fun

Let's Pretend

Activity Book

Mighty Mask

There's no limit to pretend play when you're wearing a special mask! Here is a fun-to-wear creation that you can make with your family and friends.

What You'll Need:

- ➤ large cardboard box
- ➤ yarn or string
- ➤ pencil
- ➤ scissors
- ➤ crayon or markers

- ➤ poster paints
- ➤ paintbrush
- ➤ white liquid glue
- ➤ glitter, fabric scraps, feathers, or other art materials

Here's How to Make It:

1. Cut off a flap or other rectangular-shaped piece of cardboard from a large cardboard box. To make the piece of cardboard easy to fold, the long edge should cut across the corrugated lines or ridges in the cardboard.

2. Fold the long edge of the piece of cardboard in half.

3. Hold the V-shaped piece of cardboard up to your face—you've almost got a mask! Feel on the cardboard where your eyeholes should be. Put your finger on the spot. Mark that spot with a pencil dot. Do the same with your other eye. You may want a grownup to help mark these spots for you.

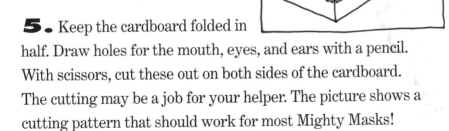

4. Follow the instructions in Step 3 to make a mark for your mouth and both ears, too.

5. Keep the cardboard folded in half. Draw holes for the mouth, eyes, and ears with a pencil. With scissors, cut these out on both sides of the cardboard. The cutting may be a job for your helper. The picture shows a cutting pattern that should work for most Mighty Masks!

6. You can cut your Mighty Mask into any shape you want: an animal face, a crown, a monster, a helmet. The picture shows you some mask ideas, but use your imagination and see what you can come up with!

229

7. Decorate the mask! Use crayons, markers, poster paints and paintbrushes, and other art materials. Glue yarn and other fabric strips to your mask for hair. Pipe cleaners make great whiskers. Cut out construction paper horns and other features. Cotton balls also make fun eyebrows, mustaches, and hair.

8. Punch a hole in the cardboard just above the earholes at the back of each side of the mask. Tie a piece of yarn or string in one of the holes. Double loop the yarn or string through the other hole so you can use it like a drawstring to tighten the mask around your face.

9. Put your mask on and bend the cardboard so that it fits comfortably around your face. Adjust the drawstring in back. Now you're ready to wear your Mighty Mask and pretend to be anything!

More Family Fun:

● Instead of using cardboard, try making Mighty Masks from paper plates! You can attach a drawstring to the back of the mask for wearing. Or you can tape the paper plate to a ruler or paper towel tube and hold the mask in front of your face.

● Make a Nosey Mask! Cut out a three-inch square piece of construction paper. Draw eyes and hair at the top of the square and a mouth and other facial features at the bottom. Use a nickel to trace a circle for the nose in the center of the paper. Use scissors to make a smaller hole in the center of the nose area. Push your nose through the hole and make sure the mask is snug on your nose. Now you have a tiny Nosey Mask that's easy to make, comfortable to wear, and very silly!

● For a mask-making challenge, try making a papier-mache mask (see page 76)!

● Go with your family to the library and check out books on masks. Mask-making is a very ancient art and has been used in plays, ceremonies, battles, and even in hunting! Find out how masks were used by African nations, by the Eskimos or Inuit peoples, by Native Americans, by the Japanese, and by the ancient Greeks. And don't forget to explore masks and Halloween!

Bag Head

Here's another fun mask idea that's simple-dimple! Make a big Bag Head and get your family and friends together for some pretend play.

What You'll Need:

- ➤ paper grocery bags
- ➤ scissors
- ➤ crayon or markers

- ➤ white liquid glue
- ➤ glitter, fabric scraps, feathers, or other art materials

Here's How to Make It:

1. Completely open up one large paper grocery bag.

2. Put it over your head so the bottom of the bag is resting on top of your head. Now you're starting to look like a real Bag Head!

3. Feel on the outside of the bag where your eyeholes should be. Put your finger on the spot. Gently mark that spot with a crayon dot. Do the same with your other eye. A grownup should help mark these spots for you.

4. The eyeholes are the only holes you really have to make, but you can be more comfortable if you follow the instructions in Step 3 to make a mark for your nose and mouth, too.

5. Draw holes for the mouth, nose, and mouth on your bag. With scissors, cut these out on just the front side of the bag. The cutting may be a job for your helper.

6. Decorate your Bag Head! Use crayons, markers, and other art materials. Glue yarn and other fabric strips to the bag for hair. Pipe cleaners make great whiskers. Cut out construction paper horns, huge ears, and other features. Cotton balls make fun eyebrows, mustaches, beards, and hair, too.

7. Now you're ready to wear your Bag Head and make-believe all day long!

More Family Fun:

- Here are some great Bag Head decorating ideas: a clown face with a red construction paper nose, an elephant with a toilet paper tube trunk and big floppy ears, a deep sea diver with paper towel tubes on the side of the mask for air, a monster face with scary horns, an outer space person with pipe cleaner antennae, a roaring lion with pipe cleaner whiskers, a princess with long pieces of beautiful yarn hair, a firefighter with a red helmet, and a picture of you!

- Make a Bag Head and a Bag Body, too! Decorate two paper grocery bags. Make one of them a Bag Head. Make the other one a matching Bag Body—a grown-up helper can cut a hole in the bottom of the bag to put your head through and a hole on each side of the bag for your arms. Decorate the Bag Body to look like a silly suit, a robot chest, a Superkid "S" costume (attach some fabric to the back for a super cape!), a clown outfit, an animal body (add a yarn tail to the back!), or a monster with creepy scales and slime.

- Make up a Bag Head play and have your family put it on for the neighborhood or your friends! Give each person in your family a part to play, gather everyone together to make Bag Heads and Bag Bodies, then practice your performance. Add music, songs, dancing, and jokes to your play. If you're playing the part of an animal, practice making animal sounds and walking or crawling like the animal you're pretending to be!

Handy Puppets

Puppets are craft projects. They're also fun ways to pretend, put on a play, retell a favorite story, or entertain your family and friends!

235

What You'll Need:

- white socks—1 or more
- wooden mixing spoons—
  1 or more
- small or large paper cups—
  1 or more
- small brown paper lunch bags—
  1 or more
- white liquid glue
- scissors
- crayon or markers
- tempera paints (optional)—
  various colors
- fabric paints (optional)—
  various colors
- paintbrush
- construction paper
- tape
- glitter, fabric scraps, feathers, or
  other art materials
- old newspapers

Here's How to Make Them:

1. There are many different ways to make hand puppets, but here are four fun ideas. Set up all the materials on a large table covered with old newspapers. Gather your family and friends together. Now you're ready to make Handy Puppets!

2. To make Spoon Puppets, you will need an old wooden mixing spoon (one that won't be used again for mixing!). Use markers or tempera paints and a paintbrush to make a face on the wide part of the spoon. You can also use white liquid glue to add yarn hair, construction paper ears, and other features. Cut out some "clothes" from fabric scraps and wrap the handle of the spoon with the material. Tape the fabric in place. Another fun idea is to cut a piece of yarn and tie the middle of the yarn snugly around the middle of the spoon handle. Trim the two ends of the yarn so they are the same length. Cut out construction paper floppy feet and tape them to the ends of the yarn. Use your imagination, and when you're done, you can hold the handle of the spoon and make your Spoon Puppet walk around and dance!

3. To make Paper Bag Puppets, you will need a small brown paper lunch bag. Use markers or crayons to make a face over the bottom flap of the bag. When you fold the bottom down flat against the rest of the bag, you can draw a mouth on both the flap and the side of the bag! You can also use white liquid glue to add yarn hair and ribbons, construction paper ears, glittery spots, and other features. Use your imagination, and when you're done, put your hand inside the bag. Bend your fingers into the bottom flap to make your Paper Bag Puppet talk and sing!

4. To make Paper Cup Puppets, you will need a paper cup. Cut a piece of construction paper as tall as the cup and long enough to more than fit around the outside of it. Use markers or crayons to make a face and body on the construction paper strip. Turn the cup upside down, then wrap the paper strip around the cup. Tightly tape the paper to the cup. You can use white liquid glue to add yarn hair and ribbons, construction paper ears and other features, glittery spots, and other items to the sides and top of the cup. On the back side of the cup, just above the bottom rim, cut two small holes, just big enough for your fingers to fit through (ask for help if you need it). When you're done, put two fingers through the holes and make your Paper Cup Puppet walk around on its funny legs!

5. To make Sock Puppets, you will need a clean white sock. Use markers or some fabric paints and a paintbrush to make a face near the toe end of the sock. Decorate the rest of the sock the same way! You can also use white liquid glue to add yarn hair and ribbons, pom-pom or button eyes, and so on. Ask a grownup to help you use a sewing needle and thread to sew on fabric pieces, buttons, and other materials to your puppet. Use your imagination, and when you're done, put the sock on over your hand and arm. Bend your fingers up and down to make your Sock Puppet talk and sing!

More Family Fun:

● Make a puppet stage for your Handy Puppets! Drape a tablecloth or sheet over a table and hide behind it. Stick your hands up over the top of the table to put on your puppet show. Put on a show for your family and friends.

● You can also cut out a large window in the side of a big cardboard box. Cut out a crawl-through opening in the back of the box. Decorate the box and turn it into a Puppet Theater! Crawl inside and stick your Handy Puppets over the bottom edge of the window to put on your puppet show.

● Make a Spoon Marionette! First, make a Spoon Puppet. Add the floppy feet and yarn legs near the end of the spoon handle (not in the middle). Tie a two-foot piece of yarn around the neck of the spoon, near the head. Tie the other end of the yarn to a ruler or paper towel tube. Hold onto the ruler or tube, stand up, and lift your puppet into the air. Hold it so that its floppy legs just touch the floor. Make it walk around and dance. You've just made a string puppet or marionette!

● Go with your family to the library and look up books on dolls, hand puppets, and marionettes. See how dolls and puppets are made by different peoples in different countries. Get some new decorating and puppet-making ideas from what you read!

Me and My Shadow

Here's how to get started making wonderful make-believe plays and stories with your very own Shadow Puppets and Shadow Box! Surprise your family and friends with this great project.

What You'll Need to Make Shadow Puppets:

- ➤ cookie cutters—use animals and people shapes
- ➤ construction paper
- ➤ plastic drinking straws, popsicle/craft sticks, or plastic silverware—1 for each puppet

- ➤ pencil
- ➤ paper punch
- ➤ scissors
- ➤ tape

Here's How to Make Them:

1. With a pencil, trace the outline of animal and people cookie cutters onto pieces of construction paper. You can also draw the outlines of anything you'd like—how about a witch, a ballerina, a space explorer, a monster, a dinosaur, an angel, or a robot?

2. Cut out the construction paper outlines with scissors.

3. Use a paper punch to punch out holes for eyes in your animal and people outlines (or carefully push the point of a pencil through the paper to poke eyeholes).

4. Tape the construction paper outlines to the tops of plastic drinking straws. You can also tape them to popsicle or craft sticks, pencils, pens, or plastic silverware.

Me and My Shadow

What You'll Need to Make a Shadow Box:

➤ medium cardboard box
➤ tracing paper or an old white sheet
➤ pencil
➤ scissors
➤ tape

➤ crayons or markers
➤ white liquid glue
➤ glitter, fabric scraps, feathers, or other art materials
➤ flashlight

Here's How to Make It:

1. Have a grownup help you cut the flaps off the top of a medium cardboard box.

2. Draw a large rectangle on the bottom of the box and have your helper cut it out with scissors. The bottom of the box should look like a TV screen!

3. Lay a piece of tracing paper inside the box, on the bottom, and make sure it more than covers the opening you cut in Step 2. You can also use a piece of an old white sheet, cut slightly larger than the opening. Tape the tracing paper or sheet to the inside bottom of the box.

4. Decorate the Shadow Box with crayons, markers, and other art materials. But don't draw anything on the screen! (The screen is the tracing paper or white sheet.)

5. Put a tablecloth or sheet over a table. Set the Shadow Box on the table so that the screen faces your audience and the open back of the box faces you.

6. The Shadow Box works best in a room that's dark or not brightly lit. Shine the bright light from a flashlight behind the box. Aim the light directly inside the box and against the screen.

7. Hold up your Shadow Puppets between the light and the screen (close to the screen, but not touching it) so that the light casts shadows on the screen. All your audience will see is the dark shadowy outlines of your puppets. Now you're ready to move the puppets around the screen area to put on a Shadow Puppet show!

More Family Fun:

● Put on a Shadow Puppet show for your family and friends! Make up your own story or play and act it out for them. You can also make your puppets dance to a story record or cassette tape.

● You can make Giant Shadow Puppets! Shine a bright light from a table lamp or flashlight on your shadow puppets. They'll cast a big shadow on any bare wall. Adjust the position of the light and the puppets until you get shadows with sharp outlines.

● In India and other Asian countries, puppet makers make beautifully detailed shadow puppets with arms and legs that really move! Follow the steps found in the Body Poser activity (see page 25) to draw different people and animal outlines on construction paper, cut around the arms and legs, and fasten these parts back on the body with brads or metal fasteners. Then you can swing the arms and legs back and forth on these special shadow puppets—make them dance and walk for your audience!

● Many countries entertain large crowds of people with beautiful shadow puppets and stages. Go with your family to the library and look up books on shadow puppets! See how shadow puppets are made and read some of the special stories they tell with their puppets. Get some new puppet-making ideas and stories from these books and share them with your family and friends.

Suitcase Relay

This is the perfect outdoor game to make your neighborhood laugh out loud as everyone plays dress-up—in a big hurry!

What You'll Need:

➤ small suitcases, gym bags, or paper sacks—2

➤ old clothes—2 complete sets of outfits, 6 or more items per outfit

➤ large outdoor play area

Here's How to Do It:

1. Get two empty suitcases, gym bags, or paper sacks.

2. Collect two complete outfits and put one set in each of your empty containers. Make the outfits completely silly and funny. Get lots of old clothes. It's important, however, to have the same number of items for each outfit. Outfit ideas: hats, earrings, bracelets, necklaces, dresses, skirts, baggy pants, old shirts, socks that don't match, belts, old shoes that don't match, water flippers, gloves, coats, scarves, and sunglasses!

3. Divide your friends and family members into two equal teams.

4. Now you're ready for the Suitcase Relay to begin! Each team lines up behind a starting line.

5. The first player in each line has to race to the other side of the yard carrying one of the suitcases, bags, or sacks.

6. That player then stops and dresses up in each of the items in the suitcase or bag.

7. Then that player must race back to his or her team, wearing the funny outfit.

8. The player must quickly undress and repack the clothes, giving them to the next person on the team.

9. Each player has to race, dress, race back, undress, and pass on outfits to the next in line until one team wins the silliest race ever!

More Family Fun:

The Suitcase Relay is an exciting way to play dress-up. It's a great game for children of all ages and grownups to play together. And it's funny to watch someone in a floppy hat, a shawl, a fake beard, a ballet tutu, a boot, and a water flipper running around the yard! Here are some more fun racing ideas:

● Try coming up with a theme for the outfits in your race. Instead of mixing up different things to wear for each team, only collect winter clothes, beach clothes, red clothes, wild clothes from the '70's— you get the idea!

● Have a team of girls dress up in boy clothes and a team of boys dress up in girl clothes!

● Have a big Neighborhood Relay Race! Each team is a family from the neighborhood, and each family can bring a complete outfit in a suitcase, gym bag, or paper sack. Have families trade outfits for even more fun.

● Have an indoor Suitcase Relay at your next Halloween party! Put together masks and outfits that form a complete Halloween costume: a fairy princess, a monster, a witch, a vampire, a tiger, or a robot. Be creative—you and your family can make different costume pieces for the race.

● Go on a Family Race Outing! Attend a track meet at a high school or college and watch the relay races. Cheer on the teams as they pass batons from one racer to another!

Magic Make-Believe TV

Now you can turn an old shoebox into a special TV. Here's everything to make "Little Red Riding Hood" and other make-believe shows!

What You'll Need:

- ➤ shoebox with lid
- ➤ plastic wrap
- ➤ construction paper
- ➤ tape, paste, or glue
- ➤ scissors

- ➤ pipe cleaners, drinking straws, or pencils
- ➤ crayons or markers
- ➤ pebbles

249

Here's How to Make It:

1. Cut a big "window" in the bottom of a shoebox. Leave about a half an inch around the edges.

2. Reach in the box and stretch a piece of plastic wrap across the inside of the window. Tape or paste it to the inside of the shoebox.

3. Cut a long, narrow slit in one side of the shoebox.

4. Set the shoebox on its side so the slit is on top.

5. Make trees, bushes, and flowers from construction paper. Tape them to the bottom of the box. Put some pebbles around the scene.

6. On the inside of the shoebox lid, draw a forest scene with Grandma's Cottage in it. Tape the top onto the box—now you've got a Magic Make-Believe TV picture from "Little Red Riding Hood."

7. To make the Big Bad Wolf and Little Red Riding Hood, draw and color them on construction paper (and any other people, birds, or animals you'd like in your scene). Cut them out and tape or paste them to a pipe cleaner, drinking straw, or long pencil.

8. Now you're ready to play with your Magic Make-Believe TV! Pass your "puppets" through the slit and move them around in your forest scene. Get your friends and family together, and act out the "Little Red Riding Hood" story. You'll be a hit!

More Family Fun:

You can tell other favorite stories, too, and make up any characters—just like on TV! Read lots of books with your family to get great story and character ideas. You can also play your favorite music tapes or CDs and have your characters sing and dance to the beat. Here are some more Magic Make-Believe TV scenes you can make:

- You on the Moon
- Creepy Monsters
- Your Friends & Family
- Your Favorite Cartoons
- Inside a Castle
- Pirates on the High Seas

- Shark Diver
- Talking and Singing Animals
- A Haunted House
- Fun on the Farm
- A Treasure-filled Cave
- Rock Concert Excitement

Family Fun

Nature &
Science

Activity Book

Feed the Birds

Whether you live in the city or in the country, one thing you'll always see is a bird perching on a building ledge or on a tree branch. Now you can help feed nature's winged wonders with these two bird feeder projects!

*What You'll Need
for a Pine Cone Feeder:*

- ➤ large pine cone
- ➤ string or cord
- ➤ scissors
- ➤ spoon
- ➤ peanut butter
- ➤ birdseed
- ➤ waxed paper

Here's How to Make It:

1. Did you know that birds love peanut butter as much as children do? It's true! This project gives birds a tasty peanut butter and birdseed treat that can't be beat. Collect all the ingredients and spread them out on a table or kitchen counter.

2. With scissors, cut
a length of string or
cord long enough to tie your
bird feeder so that it hangs from a tree
branch, porch roof, balcony, or other high place.

3. Loop one end of the string or cord around the top petals of a large pine cone. Tie it tightly in place.

4. Scoop out spoonfuls of peanut butter from a jar and pack the peanut butter in between all the petals of the pine cone.

5. Tear off a large sheet of waxed paper. Sprinkle birdseed onto the waxed paper.

6. Roll your peanut butter-covered pine cone around in the birdseed. Gently press the pine cone on top of the birdseeds so the seeds get nicely stuck in the peanut butter.

7. Hang your Pine Cone Feeder in a tree or other good bird feeding spot!

What You'll Need for a Milk Carton Feeder:

➤ empty milk carton—
  the half-gallon size
➤ stapler
➤ tape
➤ unsharpened pencil or dowel rod

➤ pipe cleaners or twist-ties—3
➤ birdseed
➤ funnel
➤ string, cord, or wire

Here's How to Make It:

1. This feeder is made from an empty half-gallon milk carton—make sure it's rinsed out and dry inside before you begin.

2. Close the spout on the milk carton and staple the carton shut along the top. Cover the top edge with tape so that the milk carton is now sealed shut.

3. Ask a grownup to cut a small hole in the middle of the ridge on the top of the milk carton with scissors. Stick a pipe cleaner or twist-tie through the hole and twist the ends together to form a loop.

4. On both the front and back sides of the milk carton, measure a spot one and one half inches from the bottom of the carton. Make a pencil mark in the center of the carton on both sides. Your helper can cut a small hole in the front and back of the carton.

5. Poke an unsharpened pencil or a dowel rod (cut to the length of a pencil) through the two holes. (A chopstick also works well.) This is the perch where the birds will sit while they eat!

6. This next step is for your grown-up helper. Measure one half inch up from the perch on the front and back sides of the milk carton and cut a small two-inch-square flap that lifts up (cuts are made on the sides and bottom edges of the square, folding up on the top edge).

7. Your helper can poke a hole with scissors through each flap and then poke a hole near the flap into the side of the milk carton. You can then stick a pipe cleaner or twist-tie through the holes and twist the ends into little balls so they will hold both flaps open.

8. Use a funnel to pour birdseed into your Milk Carton Feeder. Fill it up to just below the bottom edge of the flap doors.

9. Run string, cord, or wire through the loop at the top of the milk carton and hang your Milk Carton Feeder in a tree or other good bird feeding spot!

More Family Fun:

● Keep your bird feeders full of food! Birds get used to feeding at people-made feeders, so by helping birds find food, they'll come to depend on you. Feed the birds regularly, like you would feed a pet—give them lots of goodies throughout the year, and they will come to your special feeder every day. Ask different members of your family to take turns helping you keep the bird feeders filled.

● Go to the library with your family and check out books that help you identify different kinds of birds. Set up a bird watching spot in your home—maybe a certain window with a good view of your bird feeder. You and a family member can watch the birds and try to look up which birds are dining out on your yummy treats! Read all about your feathered friends.

● Have you ever had a pet bird at home? First, read up on all the things you'll need to take care of a pet bird. Then talk to the grownups in your family about the possibility of having a bird friend in your home!

● Go on a Family Bird Watching Outing! Find a good bird book at the library and go to a local park or forest area. See how many different kinds of birds you can spot. Look them up in your book and see if you can name them. Do you have a pair of binoculars? Lucky you—then you and your family can watch the birds close up!

Underwater Spyscope

When you make this project, you won't need a submarine or a deep-sea diving outfit to see underwater life in a stream, pond, creek, lake, or seashore!

What You'll Need:

- empty milk carton— the half-gallon size
- scissors
- rubber band— thick and sturdy
- plastic wrap or clear plastic bag
- masking tape

Here's How to Make It:

1. To make an Underwater Spyscope, start with an empty milk carton—make sure it's rinsed out and dry inside before you begin.

2. Have a grownup use scissors to cut the top and bottom off the milk carton.

3. Tear off a large sheet of plastic wrap. Stand the milk carton in the center of the wrap. (If you don't have plastic wrap, place the milk carton in a clear plastic bag. The bag needs to be larger than the milk carton.)

4. Wrap a sturdy rubber band around the bottom edge of the milk carton. Make sure the plastic wrap or bag covering the open bottom of the milk carton is stretched flat and tight, with the rubber band holding it firmly in place.

5. Pull the plastic wrap or plastic bag up the sides of the milk carton and tuck them over the top edge. Use masking tape to tape the ends of the plastic to the inside of the carton.

6. Now you're ready to use your Underwater Spyscope! Gently place the plastic-covered end of the carton into water and look inside the top of the milk carton. Hold it nice and steady or slowly move it around until you spot something swim or float by.

More Family Fun:

- Set up an Underwater Detective File! Use a notebook to record all your Underwater Spyscope explorations. Write down the date, the place where you looked into the water, and what you saw. Did you see plants in the water? Any fish, tadpoles, frogs, or turtles? Rocks, pebbles, and shells? Anything else?
- Go on a Family Water Outing! Visit a lake, river, ocean, creek, stream, or pond and bring your Underwater Spyscope to go exploring. Share your spyscope and take turns looking into the water. Have fun on top of the water by going fishing, wading, swimming, or boating. Have a picnic by the water with your family.
- Go to the library with your family and check out books on underwater life—fishes, shells, water plants, oceans, rivers, and a whole lot more! See if you can find any fish with your Underwater Spyscope. Can you find their pictures and names in the books? And here's an underwater mystery for you to solve: how do fish live underwater, how do they breathe, and what do they do when their watery homes freeze up in winter?

Flower Power

After growing beautiful flowers in your home garden, it's sad to see them wilt and die. In this project you can dry out flowers with sand and keep them beautiful...then make bouquets and paperweights with them!

What You'll Need for Sand-Dried Flowers:

➤ shoebox

➤ sand

➤ scissors

➤ freshly-picked flowers

Here's How to Make Them:

1. To make Sand-Dried Flowers, start with an empty shoebox. Fill it half full with sand.

2. Take flowers that you've just cut from the garden and use scissors to cut off all the leaves from the stems. Then trim the stems so that they're two inches long.

3. Gently press each flower into the sand in the shoe box. Space the flowers out so the petals don't touch each other.

4. Sprinkle a thin layer of sand over the flower petals until they are completely covered. For thicker flowers like roses, gently separate the petals and sprinkle sand between them.

5. Put the shoebox in a dry place like a closet or under your bed. Let the flowers dry for about two weeks.

6. Carefully tilt the box and jiggle the top layer of sand out of the box, uncovering the flowers. Gently lift out the flowers. Now you have Sand-Dried Flowers that will last and last!

What You'll Need for a Dried Flower Bouquet:

- ➤ sand-dried flowers
- ➤ plastic drinking straws
- ➤ pipe cleaners
- ➤ construction paper
- ➤ scissors
- ➤ white liquid glue

- ➤ tape
- ➤ empty juice container
- ➤ crayons or markers
- ➤ glitter, fabric scraps, feathers, or other art materials
- ➤ clay or play dough

Here's How to Make It:

1. Take a sand-dried flower and gently place the stem inside a plastic drinking straw.

2. Secure the stem and flower to the straw by wrapping a short piece of pipe cleaner around the stem and straw.

3. Cut out leaves from construction paper and use white liquid glue to attach them to the drinking straw stem.

4. Follow Steps 1–3 for your other sand-dried flowers.

5. Cut a piece of construction paper to fit the size of an empty juice container. Decorate it with designs, pictures, and special messages using crayons, markers and other other art materials. Glue the paper to the outside of the juice container.

6. Place a lump of clay or play dough on the bottom of the juice container and stick the ends of the drinking straws into the container to form a beautiful Dried Flower Bouquet!

What You'll Need
for a Dried Flower Paperweight:

➤ sand-dried flower
➤ small glass jar, with lid
➤ construction paper
➤ pencil
➤ scissors
➤ white liquid glue

Here's How to Make It:

1. Soak a small glass jar and lid in warm or hot water until the jar label peels off. Make sure the jar is rinsed out and dried off before you begin.

2. Use the jar lid to trace a circle on a piece of construction paper with a pencil. Cut out the circle and glue it to the inside of the jar lid.

3. Take a sand-dried flower and trim off most of the stem. Glue the flower to the construction paper on the inside of the jar lid. Let the glue dry.

4. Keeping the lid flat and the flower facing up, gently screw on the glass jar. You've just finished making a beautiful Dried Flower Paperweight!

More Family Fun:

- Give Dried Flower Bouquet and Dried Flower Paperweight presents to family and friends! The soft, pretty colors of your dried flowers will be great gifts for birthdays, holidays, get-well wishes, and other family times.

- Go on a Family Wildflower Outing! Go into the country and choose a few flowers to sand dry. But don't pick flowers on someone's property or in a park area! Bring along your shoebox and sand so you can start to dry the flowers right away while they're still beautiful.

- Go to the library with your family and check out books on wildflowers and other flower varieties. On your flower outing, see if you can find the pictures and names of flowers in a "flower finder" guide.

Smells-Good Ball

Here is a fun project that makes a great gift for someone special—and it smells good, too. Explore the world of good smells from nature when you make an Orange Pomander Ball!

What You'll Need:

- ➤ orange
- ➤ whole cloves
- ➤ cinnamon
- ➤ plastic bag or baggie and a twist-tie

- ➤ ribbon
- ➤ string
- ➤ scissors

267

Here's How to Make It:

1. Whole cloves have a little ball at one end and a pointed stem on the other end. Push the pointed stems of cloves into an orange. Cover the whole orange with cloves. What you'll end up with will look like a ball of cloves!

2. Put some cinnamon into a plastic bag or baggie. Place the cloves-covered orange in the bag.

3. Wrap a twist-tie around the top of the bag and shake the orange in the cinnamon.

4. Take the orange out of the bag.

5. With scissors, cut a piece of ribbon and wrap it around the length of the orange. Tie it into a knot at the top of the orange.

6. Wrap another piece of ribbon around the orange. Crisscross the first ribbon at the bottom and knot the two ribbons at the top.

7. Tie a string or another piece of ribbon to the knotted ribbons at the top of the orange.

8. Hang your Orange Pomander Ball in a closet or room to make it smell special! The orange will slowly shrink, but your ball should continue to smell great.

More Family Fun:

● Give an Orange Pomander Ball as a gift to someone special in your family! It makes closets and rooms smell wonderful. Put your ball inside a small box and wrap it up. When someone opens up the box, the great smell will delight them!

● You can collect other items and make a sweet-smelling Sachet Bag! Put dried lilac or other dried flowers into a netting bag or small cloth bag (a grownup can help you sew one up). Tie the bag at the top with pretty ribbon. You've got another great gift to make any closet or clothing drawer smell fresh and sweet!

● Smells are amazing—set up a Smelling Game for your family and friends! In small paper lunch bags, place different items that have a distinctive smell. Hold the bags shut with twist-ties. To play the game, blindfold players and have them take turns trying to guess what's inside each bag—just by smelling. Here are a few items you can collect for the Smelling Game: mint leaves, cinnamon, pepper, garlic, roses, lavender, lilac, pine needles, and coffee beans or grounds.

● Families used spicy-smelling Orange Pomander Balls in their kitchens during pioneer times to help freshen the air. Go to the library with your family and read all about pioneer families and the way they lived! There are many great pioneer stories you can read, too. Find other pioneer craft projects—like corn husk dolls—and make them with your family and friends.

● At the library, look up books on the nose and how it works. How can a nose help you smell? Find out why it's hard to taste food if you have a bad cold and a stuffy nose!

Leaf Pictures

Here are some projects that will have you look for all different kinds of leaves—look for unusual shapes, different colors, and different sizes. Happy leaf hunting!

What You'll Need:

- ➤ tree leaves—fresh ones, not ones that are dry and brittle
- ➤ cardboard
- ➤ white liquid glue
- ➤ poster paints or an ink pad
- ➤ paintbrush
- ➤ drawing paper
- ➤ old newspapers

- ➤ art smock or old clothes—an old shirt worn backwards makes a great smock
- ➤ paper plate
- ➤ straight pins
- ➤ old toothbrush
- ➤ popsicle or craft stick
- ➤ sponge
- ➤ crayons

Here's How to Make Them:

1. First, lay down lots of old newspaper or an old plastic tablecloth to protect the surface you work on.

2. To make Leaf Prints, collect leaves of many different shapes and sizes. Find the smooth side of a leaf and put white liquid glue around the edges. Glue the smooth side of the leaf to a piece

271

of cardboard and wait until it dries. Paint a thin coating of poster paint on the leaf or press the surface of the leaf onto an ink pad. Press the leaf down on a sheet of drawing paper. Hold it firmly in place, then carefully lift it off. You've made a colorful Leaf Print showing all the veins stem of the leaf! Glue more leaves to pieces of cardboard and make a beautiful Leaf Print picture.

3. To make a Leaf Stencil, place a leaf down on a sheet of drawing paper. One way to make a stencil of the leaf is to pour a little poster paint onto a paper plate and dip a sponge into the paint. Dab the paint-covered sponge all along the outer edges of the leaf and onto the drawing paper. Hold the leaf down with your fingers while you dab the sponge around the leaf. Carefully lift the leaf up and you have a stencil or outline of the leaf on the paper! Another way to make a stencil is to place a leaf down on a piece of thick cardboard and hold the different parts of the leaf down by poking straight pins

through the leaf and into the cardboard. Pour a little poster paint onto a paper plate and dip the bristles of an old toothbrush into the paint. Let the extra paint drip off the brush. Hold the brush over the leaf and carefully rub a popsicle or craft stick over the bristles. Paint will splatter over the leaf and the paper. Cover the drawing paper around the leaf with paint spatters. Let the paint dry and then remove the pins and the leaf. What a great Leaf Stencil!

4. To make a Leaf Rubbing, glue the smooth side of several leaves to a sheet of paper. The bumpy veins of the leaves should be facing up! Next, lay a sheet of white drawing paper over the sheet with the leaves. Take off the paper wrapping on a crayon and rub the paper with the side of the crayon. The veins and stems of the leaves will appear like magic! Use different crayon colors to make your Leaf Rubbing more colorful.

More Family Fun:

● Use Leaf Prints, Leaf Stencils, and Leaf Rubbings to decorate special party invitations! For a family birthday or holiday, decorate a sheet of paper with a leaf drawing and fold it in half to make a card.

● Use shelf paper and decorate it with Leaf Pictures to make great giftwrap! Wrap a special surprise present for someone in your family and show off your great Leaf Prints, Stencils, and Rubbings. Use these decorating ideas to make interesting shapes and colorful patterns all over the shelf paper.

● Go on a Family Leaf Hunt! Travel into the country or to a park and collect fresh leaves for your Leaf Picture projects. Pack a picnic lunch, take a hike, go fishing, go for a boat ride, and have a lot of fun with your family.

● When autumn comes, watch the leaves change colors and fall off the trees. Help your family rake leaves into big piles. Before you bag them up for the trash, make a leaf fort and have a leaf fight. Run and jump into a huge pile of soft, crunchy leaves!

● Go to the library with your family and check out books on trees and their leaves. On your Leaf Hunt, see if you can find the pictures and names of trees in a nature guidebook. Use the leaves and the bark of the trees to find out what kind of trees you've found. Find out why leaves change colors and fall off the trees every autumn. Learn all about the bumpy veins and lines on the leaves—what are they for? And why are leaves green? Read all about it!

World of Color

Look around you and you'll find a world of many different colors. In this project, you'll learn how to mix certain colors to make new colors!

What You'll Need:

➤ balloons—1 red, 1 yellow, 1 blue
➤ rubber bands—3
➤ scissors

➤ flashlights—
   1 is okay, but 2 or 3 is better

275

Here's How to Make It:

1. Have a grownup help you use scissors to cut a slit in each balloon. Start at the opening of the balloon and cut a straight line up to the top of the balloon.

2. Pick one balloon and stretch the balloon material over the front of a flashlight.

3. Hold the balloon in place on the flashlight with a sturdy rubber band.

4. Pick another of the colored balloons and repeat Steps 2 and 3 for attaching the balloon to another flashlight.

5. Your World of Color project works best in a dark room. Turn off all the lights and turn on one of your flashlights. Shine the color onto a wall. Pretty!

6. Now turn on the other flashlight and shine the color onto a different wall. It's also pretty!

7. Now you can experiment and play with the two colors from the different flashlights. Cross the light beams of your flashlights so the two colors shine in the same spot on the same wall. What happened? You made a new color that is a mix of your two colors. Awesome!

8. If you have a third flashlight, then you can set up the third balloon over its face and use all three in your color play. If you don't, that's no problem. Remove the rubber bands and balloons and keep switching colors.

9. You can also stretch two balloons over the same flashlight face to shine a color that combines the two balloon colors!

More Family Fun:

● Here's a quick Color Lesson for you. The three balloon colors you're using—red, yellow, and blue—are called the three "primary" colors. Mix these colors together and you get "secondary" colors. Here's how you can mix the primary colors to get secondary colors:
— Blue + Yellow = Green
— Red + Blue = Purple
— Red + Yellow = Orange
● Make a Rainbow Light Show! Use three flashlights and stretch

a different primary-colored balloon over each of the flashlight faces. Cut or poke many small holes about the size of a dime in the bottom of a paper grocery bag. Turn off all the lights and turn on the three flashlights. You and two other people can hold the flashlights inside the open paper bag and aim the bottom of the bag at the walls or ceiling. Let the light shine through the holes. Wave the flashlights back and forth and let the colors mix through the holes. You've made a beautiful Rainbow Light Show—bring all your family and friends into the room to see it!

● Make a colorful Paper Plate Face! Draw eyes, nose, and mouth shapes in the center of a paper plate. Cut them out. Turn off all the lights and shine one or more color flashlights through the holes to shine your face onto the wall or ceiling!

● Try this fun color experiment: The Mysterious Green Shamrock! Have a grownup help you draw a shamrock shape on a sheet of red construction paper. Cut it out and tape or paste it to a white sheet of paper. Now, stare at the red shamrock while you count up to fifteen (Count, "one shamrock, two shamrocks, three shamrocks, four shamrocks…"). When you get to fifteen, quickly turn the paper over and stare at the white sheet. Keep staring and soon you'll see a mysterious green shamrock on the sheet of paper. Green is the complimentary color of red, so staring at red long enough will make your eyes see green!

● Go to the library with your family and check out books on primary colors, secondary colors, complimentary colors, light, and rainbows! Find out the wonderful way your eyes pick up and see colors.

Green Thumb Projects

Both plants and children grow big and tall! Here are two fun projects you and your family will enjoy doing together to explore the amazing world of growing things.

What You'll Need for a Colorful Celery Stalk:

➤ celery stalk with leaves
➤ knife
➤ small drinking glasses—2

➤ food coloring or Color Magic dye (see page 59)—2 colors
➤ spoon

Here's How to Make It:

1. This project will show you how a plant soaks up water through its roots. The water travels all around the plant through tiny "tubes" that are inside the plant. It takes a little time for water to travel through a plant, so set up this project just before you go to bed. When you wake up, you'll find a big surprise!

2. Have a grownup use a knife to trim off the bottom part of a celery stalk that still has its leaves on it.

3. Make a slice up the center of
the celery, from the base almost up to the leaves.

4. Fill two small drinking glasses almost two-thirds full with water.

5. Add a different color of food coloring or Color Magic dye to
each glass of water. Add enough coloring or dye to make
each color dark. Red and blue are strong colors that are good to use
in this project.

6. Slide the two glasses of colored water together. Put one side of
the split celery stalk into one glass and the other side into the other
glass. Make sure both sides of the stalk are down into the colored
water.

7. Let the celery stalk soak up the colored water overnight.
What surprise will you find when you check this project the next
morning? Now you know that water travels up and through plants.
Show your family and friends what you made!

What You'll Need
for an Egg Carton Seed Starter:

- egg carton
- seeds—flowers, vegetables, and herbs
- pen or pencil
- old newspapers
- spoon
- potting soil

- water
- scissors
- shoebox (without lid)
- aluminum foil
- clear plastic bag
- twist-tie

Here's How to Make It:

1. Here's a great mini-greenhouse for sprouting seeds. Get young plants growing indoors just before the danger of frost is over. Then you can plant them outside! Start with an egg carton, and cut off the top with scissors.

2. Use a pen or pencil and poke a small water drainage hole in the bottom of each cup in the egg carton.

3. Lay out some old newspapers on your work surface. Spoon potting soil into each egg cup in the carton—fill each cup two-thirds full with soil.

4. Plant several flower, vegetable, or herb seeds into each cup. Follow planting instructions on the package for how deep you should plant each seed.

5. A grownup can help you mark the side of each egg carton cup with a pen or pencil to label what kind of seeds you planted.

6. Line an empty shoebox with aluminum foil, then put the egg carton into the shoebox.

7. Now you can water the seeds in the egg cups—but don't overwater them! Use a spoon and add about three to four spoonfuls of water to moisten the potting soil in each cup.

8. Put the shoebox into a clear plastic bag and seal it shut with a twist-tie. (Please keep plastic bags away from small children!) Put your Egg Carton Seed Starter in a dark, warm place (like a closet or under your bed).

9. Check your seed starter every day to see if your seeds are sprouting. When you see the new green shoots poking up above the potting soil, take off the plastic bag and give the bag to a grownup to recycle. Keep watering your seedlings and put them in a sunny place.

10. When your seedlings get big, transplant them to other containers. Plant them outside when the weather's right. Good job—you've got quite a Green Thumb!

More Family Fun:

- Go to the library with your family and check out books on different kinds of flowers, vegetables, and herbs. See if you can name the different parts of a flower, like the roots, petals and stem. See what kinds of seeds grow best where you live. What are your favorite flowers? What vegetables do you like to eat? Do you know that herbs make the food you eat more yummy and tasty? Make a list of your favorite plants, draw pictures of them, and show them to your family!

- Plants make great gifts—make a Fancy Potted Plant for someone special! Take a clean clay flowerpot and decorate it with sponge pieces and a paintbrush dipped in acrylic paints. Draw designs, pictures and special greetings like, "Happy Birthday, Mom!" Put potting soil in the pot and add one of your Egg Carton Seed Starter plants. Wrap pretty ribbon or yarn around the rim of the pot and tie a big bow.

- You are also a special growing thing! Make a Grow Chart and keep a record of how tall you're growing. Cut construction paper into strips about three inches wide. Tape the strips together to form a long strip of paper. Decorate the paper with crayons, markers and other art materials, but leave one side undecorated. A grownup can help you tape the Grow Chart on a wall in your bedroom or on a door. Your helper can hold a yardstick or tape measure and make numbered inch marks on the chart. Now stand with your back to the chart and let your helper make a colorful mark where the top of your head reaches—that's how tall you are now! Write the date down beside the mark. Keep making new marks at different dates.

Detective Kit

Look closely at your fingertips. Each finger has many tiny lines in it (called loops, whorls, and arches). Everybody in the world has a different set of fingerprints, and here's how you can study them!

What You'll Need:

- ➤ cornstarch
- ➤ very soft feather or brush
- ➤ pencil
- ➤ fine sandpaper
- ➤ paper or index cards
- ➤ clear tape

Here's How to Make It:

1. To start a Fingerprint File, use sheets of paper or index cards. Write the name of the person you're fingerprinting at the top of the paper or card. Then write the date, your name, which finger you're printing (like "thumb, left hand" or "middle finger, right hand"), and which type of fingerprint (loop, whorl, or arch—see the picture for each kind of pattern). Don't forget to leave room on the paper or card for the actual fingerprint!

2. To make a fingerprint, take a pencil and rub it back and forth on a sheet of paper until the marking on the paper becomes very dark from the pencil lead (called graphite). One by one, have your family members and your friends place one of their fingers on the

sheet of paper and roll it
back and forth in the graphite.
Then have the person place the finger on your Fingerprint File
paper or card. Roll the finger once from one side to the other while
pressing down on the paper. This will leave a graphite picture of the
fingerprint for your file! Protect the fingerprint by putting a piece
of clear tape over the fingerprint.

3. Now you're ready for another way to be a fingerprint
detective. First, you need to know that there is a small amount of oil
on everyone's fingertips (the oil helps keep our skin smooth). When
we touch something, we leave an invisible fingerprint on the surface
of objects. Go up to a mirror or glass window and gently press your
finger on the hard surface. You can faintly see your fingerprint on
the surface. (Wipe the window clean when you're done!)

4. To take a fingerprint from a smooth surface, you will need to use a light dusting of (a) cornstarch sprinkled on a dark surface (like a cookie jar or table top) or (b) graphite powder sprinkled on a light or clear surface (like light colors or glass). Corn starch is available in grocery stores. You can make dark graphite powder by lightly sanding the tip of a lead pencil into a cup. Sprinkle a very small amount of cornstarch or graphite powder over an area you've just touched. Use a very soft feather or brush and gently brush the cornstarch or graphite powder over the fingerprint area until you can clearly see it. Brush off the extra powder or gently blow it off the surface. Lift the fingerprint off the surface by putting a piece of clear tape over the fingerprint. Press the tape down over the print, then lift the tape up and tape it down in your Fingerprint File.

More Family Fun:

● See if you can find fingerprints on other smooth surfaces, like a car door or a drinking glass that someone's already touched. Play detective and dust the surfaces for fingerprints (cornstarch for dark surfaces, graphite powder for light or clear surfaces). Find a fingerprint, lift it with tape, and place it in your Fingerprint File. Try to match it with the fingerprints in your file. Did someone in your family make it? Gather your family together—you can all use a magnifying glass to look closely at the fingerprints to do some real detective work.

● Make a
Fingerprint Painting!
Pour a little bit of
poster paint into a
cup (or put different

colors in different cups), dip your fingertip into the paint, rub your
finger back and forth on a piece of scratch paper, then make a good,
clean fingerprint on a good sheet of paper. You can make patterns or
designs with your fingerprints, or make Fingerprint People by
drawing a hat on your fingerprint, little eyes, a mouth, and feet!
Use your imagination.

● Use graphite powder, a washable stamp pad, or poster paint to
make prints of other parts of your body that have lines on them!
Your toes, feet, elbows, and palms all have special lines and patterns
that only you have—no one else in the world has fingerprints,
toeprints, footprints, elbowprints, or palmprints like yours! That
proves how special you really are.

● Go to the library with your family and check out books on
fingerprints and fingerprinting! Find out how detectives, police, the
FBI, and other investigators use fingerprints to help solve crimes.

Windy Weather Center

Aren't you glad you
don't have a lot of weather
inside your house?
(Imagine having a big
windstorm in your bedroom!) But you do have weather outside, and
here's a great way you can tell which direction the wind is blowing.

What You'll Need:

- empty yogurt container and top
- unsharpened pencil with eraser
- plastic drinking straw
- scissors
- thin cardboard

- straight pin
- glue
- posterboard
- compass
- crayons or markers

Here's How to Make It:

1. To make a Windy Weather Vane, start with an empty
yogurt container—make sure it has been rinsed out and is dry
inside before you begin.

288

2. Have a grownup use scissors to punch a hole in the center of the container bottom.

3. Push an unsharpened pencil through the hole so that the eraser end sticks up outside the container.

4. Cut a small triangle and another triangle a little bigger from a piece of thin cardboard. Decorate both sides of the triangles with crayons or markers.

5. Have your helper cut slits into both ends of a plastic drinking straw. The slits on both ends should line up together.

6. Slide the two cardboard triangles into the slits in the drinking straw—one at each end. The smaller triangle should point like an arrow away from the straw. The larger triangle is the back part of the arrow and should point into the straw (see the picture on page 288).

7. Now your helper can push a straight pin through the center of the straw and into the eraser. The straw should spin around easily.

8. Glue the yogurt container lid to the center of a piece of cardboard. Use a compass to help mark the directions North, South, East, and West on the four sides of the cardboard with crayons or markers.

9. To make your Windy Weather Vane heavier (so it doesn't blow over in a good wind), place a lump of clay or play dough on top of the lid. Now you can snap the yogurt container onto the lid.

10. Set the weather vane outside in an open space where the wind will spin it. Use a compass to find North and turn your vane that way—see which direction the wind is blowing!

More Family Fun:

● Make a Rain Gauge! To see how much rain fell during a day, take an empty tin can and set it outside. After a rainfall, dip a ruler into the can and the wet part will tell you how much rain fell. Empty the can and you're ready for the next downpour. Write down your wind direction and rainfall measurements in a special Weather Notebook!
● Go to the library with your family and check out books on weather stations, weather forecasting, weather instruments, and weather maps. Learn all about the different words and symbols TV weatherpersons use on their weather maps!
● The best thing to do in the wind is kite flying, so go on a **Family Kite Outing!** Make or buy a kite and head to the park, beach, or an open field and let your kite fly proudly. Take turns running and getting the kite aloft, then holding the string and making it soar higher and higher into the sky! Make a special tail for your kite by using markers or fabric paints on strips of white cloth. Have all family members write their names on a part of the tail and draw family pictures!